AF750854

Computer-Mediated Communication

Edited by Indrakshi Dey

Published in London, United Kingdom

IntechOpen

Supporting open minds since 2005

Computer-Mediated Communication
http://dx.doi.org/10.5772/intechopen.92467
Edited by Indrakshi Dey

Contributors
Zarif Bin Akhtar, A.K.M. Jahangir Alam Majumder, Charles B. Veilleux, Shephard Pondiwa, Umayra El Nabahany, Margaret Phiri, Suzanna Schmeelk, Byeong-hee Roh, Jehad Ali, Kevin Koidl, Joan Adria Ruiz-de-Azua, Anna Calveras, Adriano Camps, Andreia Filipa Valada Pereira Artífice, João Sarraipa, Ricardo Jardim-Goncalves

© The Editor(s) and the Author(s) 2022
The rights of the editor(s) and the author(s) have been asserted in accordance with the Copyright, Designs and Patents Act 1988. All rights to the book as a whole are reserved by INTECHOPEN LIMITED. The book as a whole (compilation) cannot be reproduced, distributed or used for commercial or non-commercial purposes without INTECHOPEN LIMITED's written permission. Enquiries concerning the use of the book should be directed to INTECHOPEN LIMITED rights and permissions department (permissions@intechopen.com).
Violations are liable to prosecution under the governing Copyright Law.

Individual chapters of this publication are distributed under the terms of the Creative Commons Attribution 3.0 Unported License which permits commercial use, distribution and reproduction of the individual chapters, provided the original author(s) and source publication are appropriately acknowledged. If so indicated, certain images may not be included under the Creative Commons license. In such cases users will need to obtain permission from the license holder to reproduce the material. More details and guidelines concerning content reuse and adaptation can be found at http://www.intechopen.com/copyright-policy.html.

Notice
Statements and opinions expressed in the chapters are these of the individual contributors and not necessarily those of the editors or publisher. No responsibility is accepted for the accuracy of information contained in the published chapters. The publisher assumes no responsibility for any damage or injury to persons or property arising out of the use of any materials, instructions, methods or ideas contained in the book.

First published in London, United Kingdom, 2022 by IntechOpen
IntechOpen is the global imprint of INTECHOPEN LIMITED, registered in England and Wales, registration number: 11086078, 5 Princes Gate Court, London, SW7 2QJ, United Kingdom
Printed in Croatia

British Library Cataloguing-in-Publication Data
A catalogue record for this book is available from the British Library

Additional hard and PDF copies can be obtained from orders@intechopen.com

Computer-Mediated Communication
Edited by Indrakshi Dey
p. cm.
Print ISBN 978-1-83969-309-0
Online ISBN 978-1-83969-310-6
eBook (PDF) ISBN 978-1-83969-311-3

For EU product safety concerns:
IN TECH d.o.o., Prolaz Marije Krucifikse Kozulić 3, 51000 Rijeka, Croatia, info@intechopen.com or visit our website at intechopen.com.

We are IntechOpen, the world's leading publisher of Open Access books

Built by scientists, for scientists

5,600+
Open access books available

138,000+
International authors and editors

170M+
Downloads

156
Countries delivered to

Our authors are among the
Top 1%
most cited scientists

12.2%
Contributors from top 500 universities

CLARIVATE ANALYTICS BOOK CITATION INDEX INDEXED

WEB OF SCIENCE™

Selection of our books indexed in the Book Citation Index (BKCI)
in Web of Science Core Collection™

Interested in publishing with us?
Contact book.department@intechopen.com

Numbers displayed above are based on latest data collected.
For more information visit www.intechopen.com

Meet the editor

Dr. Indrakshi Dey is currently an assistant professor in the Department of Electronic Engineering, National University of Ireland, Maynooth, Ireland, an adjunct assistant professor at Trinity College Dublin, Ireland, and an associate investigator at the CONNECT Center for Future Communications and Networks. She received an MSc in Wireless Communications from the University of Southampton, UK, in 2010, and a Ph.D. in Electrical Engineering from the University of Calgary, Canada, in 2015. She has authored twenty journal papers, four research monographs, five book chapters, two books, and eighteen conference papers. Presently, Dr. Dey is involved in developing propagation link models for full-duplex Internet of Things, intra-body and inter-body communication, and underwater acoustic and probabilistic quantum communication networks.

Contents

Preface

If different forms of human communication are mediated through a network of computers, the communication techniques can be grouped as Computer-mediated Communications (CMC). These techniques can be synchronous or asynchronous, point-to-point, or point-to-multipoint. How CMC techniques can change the processes and results of social interaction was the principal focus of early research. CMC techniques have different effects than non-mediated, face-to-face human communications in terms of how people identify with themselves, form and manage impressions, develop and maintain relationships with other people, build communities, and collaborate, decide, and communicate when they are separated by distance in space or by time. When CMC techniques were first introduced, there were challenges to be mitigated, like lack of socio-contextual information and lack of real applications that can be used for the benefit of the greater good. However, with rights to open access of information and human data and maturity of technology capable of realizing emerging applications, CMC techniques can be applied in various scenarios to help people communicate, collaborate over distance, estimate and predict risks and outcomes, interact within group processes, address issues, and remotely manage situations.

This book investigates the present trends in research in CMC techniques through the perspective of four different application scenarios. The first application scenario is telecommunication networks that involve the exchange of text, audio, and/or video messages between people separated by space and time. The second application scenario is smart health. The idea is to collect data from portable sensors and deliver it to a central gateway for automated immediate diagnosis, real-time risk analysis, generating preventive alerts, and using CMC techniques for activating appropriate action if necessary. The third application scenario is the case where audio and video recordings and platforms like Microsoft Teams are used to deliver content for learning over a distance. The fourth and final application scenario is the human-computer interaction-mediated scenario for elevating experience in environments like gaming or dyadic interaction between familiar people.

Indrakshi Dey
Electronic Engineering,
National University of Ireland, Maynooth,
Maynooth, Ireland

Section 1

Communication Networks

Chapter 1

A Theoretical Concept to Increase the Trustworthiness of Online and Offline Debates with Real-Time AI Speech Analytics

Kevin Koidl

Abstract

Debates are an essential democratic institution in danger by the rise of Social Media. The advent of Fake News often referred to as the 'crisis of trust', has led to a substantial increase in debates that blend online and offline. It can be argued that blended approaches are not directly linked to increasing trustworthiness in the debate. To overcome this trust crisis and increase the reliability in debates, we introduce the HELIOSPHERE concept that seeks to use technological advances, such as Artificial Intelligence and Augmented Reality, to create a more fair, inclusive and transparent debate. The critical component for inclusiveness is Augmented Reality technology and 3D camera technology to hybridise the online and offline debating space and ensure that anyone who cannot be present can engage with the debate. For transparency and fairness, a key indicator of trust, an Artificial Intelligence dashboard is introduced to analyse and visualise speaking time, speaker gender, topic relatedness, bias detection sentiment in Real-Time. This work presents the overall theoretical concept focusing on academic and technical concepts to support reliable communication within debates.

Keywords: Real-Time AI, Speech to Text, NLP, Analytics, communication, media, physical spaces

1. Introduction

Modern society depends on open and fair debates to shape democracy. For a debate to be successful, it is essential that different viewpoints can be addressed and discussed. This requires fairness and trust. Traditional locations for debates are Town Halls, TV Debates and Universities. Debates guide public policy and serve to increase the legitimacy of measures since they have originated from citizens or are supported by citizen groups [1]. Debates often consist of a group of citizens with a large amount of information, which then deliberate on public policy directions, intending to reach consensus towards specific recommendations [2]. Naturally, citizen groups have been identified as a promising effort to promote deliberative democracy [3]. Research predominantly focuses on such debates and how the participants are transformed through the experience.

"[...] in the long term, deliberative civic engagement efforts could transform not only their participants but also the larger public. Those participating in, engaged with, or captivated by such actions should report stable (or rising) public trust levels and signs of reduced civic neglect" [4].

"[...] in the long term, deliberative civic engagement efforts could transform not only their participants but also the larger public. Those participating in, engaged with, or captivated by such efforts should report stable (or rising) levels of public trust and signs of reduced civic neglect" [5–7].

In other words, public debates can be considered a remedy to political distrust. Studies focused on how such debates can promote social learning [8], change the participant's preferences [9]. Such debates are often seen as the most advanced method to institutionalise deliberative democracy [10].

Currently, a general agreement has been reached that small circle debate, also defined as mini-publics, is one component of deliberative democracy [11–13]. The possibility of utilising the emerging information and communication technologies for new ways of citizen participation since network technologies allow for ease of access to civic involvement in politics [14, 15]. Additional benefits have been identified in terms of democratic discussions among people [16, 17], such as eliminating physical and social barriers that have a restrictive impact on offline mini-publics [18]. Even Supreme Court Justice Anthony Kennedy pointed out that discussions nowadays do not happen in streets and parks and instead happen via electronic media. Therefore, he reiterated the publics ability to participate in discussions would change due to changes in communication technologies [19]. Thus, one of the main challenges is how to 'translate' the traditional public forum into a more modern technological environment. Yet, at the same time, preserve the most important ideals of public forums such as insurance that speakers have access to a broad audience, equal time of speaking and that the public has a shared exposure to diverse views and opinions.

Recent events about the global COVID-19 pandemic have proven that in the presence of a worldwide mass lockdown of society for a considerable period, a scalable online deliberative platform would become increasingly more critical for the preservation of democracy and for decision making, which affects both local and global diverse communities and interests. Yet, most research and initiatives on online deliberative publics do not contemplate the effects new media concepts, such as Social Media and online forums, have on how and where debates are conducted. It can be argued that both online and offline deliberation can lead to further polarisation [19]. Specifically, with the advent of Social Media Platforms, the overall debating landscape has resulted in a complex global plethora of constantly changing media interactions affecting the individual citizen. New media experiences that are user-driven new phenomena have emerged, known as Filter Bubbles [20] and Echo Chambers [21]. Both phenomena create a distorted view of the overall reality in which the debate is held. This became very clear during the last US elections in which the primarily east coast based liberal press debated a for them sure candidate, Hillary Clinton, hence creating an Echo Chamber. The debate was biased entirely towards the opinion of the liberal news outlets creating a distorted view of the overall US picture [22]. This phenomenon is propelled by Filter Bubbles, in which content of interest is prioritised, leaving out the range of friends that are of a different opinion [23]. The overall challenge is a constant misunderstanding or artificial bias within online spaces that facilitate debate. On the flip side, however, it is not easy to scale a physical discussion and organise it in a transparent, inclusive and fair manner. About fairness, the concept of bias plays a vital key and is often misunderstood. Biases within debates are inherently necessary because it represents the opinion or value system of the debating parties. However, it is essential for a debate that these biases are known to everyone.

A further challenge in modern digital or physical debates is Fake News. This topic has played a significant role in the last US election and has become known as the Cambridge Analytica scandal. Fake News's core is beyond simply posting or circulating false news, but the danger lies more in the nuance of its influence. In the form of ads, news articles can subtly influence members of society to vote for a different party and have become known as the Cambridge Analytica scandal [24]. Therefore, it can be argued that Fake News is endangering an open and honest democratic process due to the lack of reflection and debate around the opinions of the members of a democratic society.

Furthermore, it can be argued that the emergence of Deep Fake, which uses high-end AI technology to create a falsified video, which is close to impossible for a human to identify as false. It will lead to even more distrust in media in general and further weaken the public's trust in the modern media landscape [25]. Similarly, behavioural and attention economics in the digital context shape media content, creating shorter and addictive content rather than a deep and reflective one that requires more time.

This publication introduces the HELIOSPHERE concept to introduce a participant focused, fair, sustainable and technologically advanced debating concept to empower a transparent, inclusive and honest debate. It is about inclusiveness by facilitating a hybridisation of the online and offline, digital and physical, real and virtual. HELIOSPHERE, therefore, forms a conceptual and theoretical base for modern debates that empowered by modern media technology without weakening the core of the discussion: honest, respectful and trustworthy communication between citizens. At its core, HELIOSPHERE empowers online, and offline debates with sophisticated Machine Learning analytics that results in a media value chain that supports the moderation of a discussion to ensure the debate is transparent, inclusive and fair. A pertinent point in the current environment is the ability of HELIOSPHERE to be functional and help citizens during massive societal lock-downs due to its online nature and ability to include people even in the most stringent social distancing environments.

2. Theoretical concept

The HELIOSPHERE is an inclusive, transparent and fair debating platform that addresses the lack of trust in public, online and offline debates to support the democratic process of modern society. It implements an easy-to-apply solution that can be used in any public setting, whether entirely online or as a hybrid concept, both offline and online and with minimal effort. The main component about trust is the AI-supported real-time debate analytics solution, which supports both the moderation and the offline/online audience in identifying and adjusting to elements of debates that create bias, manipulation, monopolisation etc. Participants can share, design and validate the debate with relevant content. HELIOSPHERE utilises Machine Learning models trained on datasets collected from already held debates and speeches that enable the debate to become more transparent and fairer and data gathered from media, political and other resources (see below the data engine section). The platform is not limited to a particular language, border limitations. It includes multilingual real-time modules, Cross-Border Content Rights, Data Privacy embedded from the start, Freedom of Speech to understand how meaningful debates can increase the trust in the political and democratic communication process in modern society.

In other words, public debates can be considered a remedy to political distrust. Studies focused on how such debates can promote social learning [8], change the participant's preferences [9]. This type of debate is viewed as the most advanced method to institutionalise deliberative democracy [10].

To increase transparency, inclusiveness and fairness during the debate, the HELIOSPHERE visualisation focuses on the following analytics results:

- Information on the number and duration of male or female contributions may help the moderator to find a balance in this respect.

- Statements can be weighted according to their overall popularity, based on the results of the analytics before the debate - not to support these statements and to give the impression they would be more plausible but to put the finger on it and give the speaker the chance to react to this fact.

- Most importantly, the fact-checker provides an analysis of the plausibility of any statement so that the moderator or any participant in the debate can pick up a line and bring it up again to avoid that populists win a debate based on good rhetoric alone.

Sensible guidelines support moderators in making fair use of this information to ensure that they will increase fairness and reason throughout the debate rather than making it easier for any speaker to win an argument through clever manipulation. The HELIOSPHERE system will continue to learn and monitor the topic's coverage and identify when the time has come to re-open the debate or have a new debate on the subject based on significant recent developments. In the following sections, we describe the platform architecture and its components.

3. The heliosphere architecture

The HELIOSPHERE Engine Architecture is developed in a modular manner to support transparent and inclusive debates [26]. The architecture has four main goals: data collection, machine model training and deployment of the tools, visualisation during and after debates. There are three main parts of the platform: Data Engine, Machine Learning Engine and Customizable Visualisation Engine.

3.1 The heliosphere data engine

The HELIOSPHERE Data Engine is responsible for storing and pre-processing all the collected data, including Data collected from the debates themselves. During the debate, an automatic speech to text module transforms the speech into text. Additionally, data collected from other sources, including related initiatives, historical events, business/academic, political entities, published speeches (video, audio, transcripts), documents from governmental and non-governmental institutions (including UN, UNESCO, EU Council, EU Parliament, National Legislative Bodies, WTO, World Bank, IMF) and NGO's published data. Data collected from publicly available content from TV and print media, publicly available social media postings (Twitter, Facebook, Reddit, YouTube, Steemit or any relevant or future social media platform) related to the debate topics are pre-processed and stored within the data engine.

Since the data collected is heterogeneous, it requires collecting raw data, which is parsed, pre-processed and standardised to be compliant with reusability and compatibility. The raw data is pre-processed, prepared and annotated before including it in the data storage engine continuously. As such, the technological solution would necessitate a distributed environment, such as Hadoop[1] system to provide real-time queries and interactive aggregations even with tens of thousands of data points. The data engine is structured to provide fast (1–2 seconds query access) to the data, requested either by the ML and visualisation engine, third parties through the APIs or other services. Furthermore, specific blockchain smart contracts need to be included in the Data engine to guarantee data privacy.

To mitigate and recognise fake, deep fake information and illegal content, the engine ensures the utilisation of blockchain technology to provide traceability, transparency, and decentralisation. As such, Blockchain implementation offers reliable support for verifying both the content and its source. Different actors, people involved in the debate, can access a public blockchain where data is tagged and can, in turn, define a 'Debunker Community' and can give opinions on the content during the debate. These opinions may be registered in the tamper-free, publicly accessible ledger. However, complex queries on the blockchain's data cannot be directly supported by the blockchain itself due to performance and scalability issues. HELIOSPHERE, therefore, provides an interface between the blockchain and the Data Engine so that the Data Engine can retrieve the data on the blockchain to support complex data analysis efficiently. The Data Engine will also store the result of complex aggregation queries in the blockchain. This ensures the results of the study available to the actors of the debate and immutable.

3.2 The heliosphere machine learning engine

The HELIOSPHERE Machine Learning Engine is responsible for providing the AI models used for various components. The deployment of algorithms/models rely on three main parts - (1) data queried from the Data engine, which are needed for the training and testing phases, (2) the neural and ML models, candidates for each component, and finally (3) the code required to implement everything together. The engine's iterative nature and its way of functioning - a neural model, is proposed, trained on available data. All suitable candidate models are compared and evaluated, which informs selecting the most suitable one for the task at hand. Then the model is deployed for the next debate or innovation cycle.

The engine utilises both tensorflow[2] and pytorch[3] options, allowing further Enrichment for the model building (code phase). The models can be accessed through internal API calls or the APIs of the partners. Based on the models and structure, several main components will be available, for instance:

The Speech-to-text component is a real-time component and used during the debate as an automatic tool for closed captioning and improving the speech-to-text in case errors occur during the live transcription. This separates the audio stream into segments of a predefined length with a buffer option for uninterruptible service. Each segment denoising and feature extraction is performed (which comprises the pre-processing phase), leading to the acoustic model generation and the language model. A speaker diarisation tool is used for discovering different speakers and enabling the segmenting of the incoming audio stream into individual speaker profiles. This allows a normalisation of the predictive models for each speaker. Since debates are often situated in a noisy environment, a separate voice frequency from background sounds before submitting it to the speech-to-text engine is identified. The speech-to-text conversion distinguishes between different speakers and currently disregards background music, fast or garbled speech, interruptions (such

[1] https://hadoop.apache.org/

[2] https://www.tensorflow.org/

[3] https://pytorch.org/

as applause, crowd cheering, or other speakers butting in). The final output is a textual format saved into the Data engine module with the required annotations for each debate and each participant. The output is also available for visualisation on the dashboard.

The Language Model specifies all word combinations with semantic meaning formed and their probability of occurrence. The Dictionary is required to integrate phonemes and transcriptions of different pronunciations for a word. The level of granularity characterises it for transcription in phonemes.

Speech-to-Speech translation is implemented as a hybrid speech-to-speech system for three main reasons:

1. There is no sufficient amount of parallel audio data to allow researchers and developers to train efficient end-to-end speech translation systems. Decomposing the speech-to-speech translation tasks into smaller tasks can take advantage of the lower training data requirements for each of the underlying functions compared to the end-to-end model.

2. Exploiting different components in a distributed fashion is computationally more efficient at training time, allows for better controllability and is easier to upgrade.

3. A composite system can share components from other subsystems of the HELIOSPHERE ecosystem.

The ASR and Synthesis components are shared with other subsystems of the HELIOSPHERE ecosystem. As such, we will focus on developing the MT system and developing communication protocols with different methods to ensure a coherent speech-to-speech MT component. To potentially synchronise an avatar with the text, intermediate post-processing is conducted to generate a set of visemes and timecode based on the translated text's phonemes. We will also consider this post-processing as part of the MT component.

The MT component has two objectives: (i) to provide inclusiveness via translation for users that conduct the debates in different languages and (ii) to provide inclusiveness via translation of the debates into English to generate content in the correct language and format for the analytics component. We apply three different MT systems to handle speech (in the form of audio input) and text: (i) a text-to-text bilingual MT to translate from and to English; (ii) a text-to-text multilingual MT that encapsulates multiple languages, including English, aiming to provide translation between language pairs for which bilingual parallel data is not available and (iii) a multimodal, speech-text-to-text translation system that exploits both speech and text to improve the text translation.

HELIOSPHERE exploits neural MT approaches using open and free software, such as OpenNMT[4] and Marian[5], which provide speech-to-text and multi-source translation. The goal is to improve our models' efficiency and the architecture of our system to make it suitable for an HPC ecosystem. The third type of the MT-system mentioned above systems conducts a second stage translation similar to automatic post-editing systems. It uses two types of inputs -- speech (user-generated audio) and text (result from ASR or the first-stage translation) -- and produces an improved version of the initial translation. Following positive examples from domain-adapted MT, gender-aware MT, and others, we will develop a

[4] https://opennmt.net/

[5] https://marian-nmt.github.io/

context-aware MT conditioned on the debate's topic. HELIOSPHERE provides additional context information regarding the subject and the speakers that can help the translation system generate better translations. In this way, we will ensure a coherent translation and reduce biases. The MT component has a distributed architecture. It operates in real-time and adapts to traffic through a series of scaling up/down policies that maintain the required number of resources for optimal performance. It is accessed via a set of API calls that allow human users and other components of the HELIOSPHERE ecosystem to interact with the MT component efficiently. This reduces the efforts for connecting the MT component has to the other components of the HELIOSPHERE ecosystem. We envisage a request handling fleet that will listen and store MT requests in a queue; another system will consume requests from the queue and invoke the requested action; once the action is completed, a response will be sent directly endpoint provided with the initial request.

Other components interact with the MT Pipeline via internal API calls. The viseme and timecode post-processing, as any post-processing, are invoked if necessary and is assumed to be a part of the MT action.

Natural Language Processing Component extracts features, including tokenization, word segmentation, Part of Speech (POS) tagging, parsing techniques, named entity recognition, n-gram language model, emotional and sentiment analysis, text/debate summarisation, structural relations modelled using semantic compositionality, K-means clustering, Affinity Propagation, Latent Dirichlet Analysis, Events analysis. Established toolkits such as nltk[6], gensim[7], SpaCy[8], pattern[9], and others will be used.

Additional NLP endpoints are specifically targeted towards the real-time analysis of live discussion streams applicable in the HELIOSPHERE platform. These include:

- a pipeline for unsupervised training of domain-dependent, aspect-based sentiment analysis classifiers: this allows topic-specific sentiment analyzers to be easily pre-trained in advance of a heliosphere-event. During an event, these classifiers will extract and quantify observed opinion-aspect pairs in real-time relevant to the topic of the discussion.

- stance detection identifies and tracks on which side of the argument actors in the discussion are situated. This not only allows for the visualisation of (possibly shifting trends in) the stance of the participants but also serves to pinpoint bias in the discussion, for example, when sure sides of the argument are given an unproportionate amount of time during the debate (e.g. majority vs. minority voices).

- level-of-disagreement detection: Internet pioneer and essayist Paul Graham identified seven types of disagreement, which are most often used in online arguments, ranging from name-calling (level 1) to refuting the central point.

The HELIOSPHERE Visualisation Engine's primary purpose is to provide visualisation and interactivity capabilities to moderators, participators, and audiences.

[6] https://www.nltk.org/
[7] https://radimrehurek.com/gensim/
[8] https://spacy.io/
[9] https://www.clips.uantwerpen.be/pattern

The goal is to ensure transparency and fairness during a debate. Through a customizable visualisation, the analysis generated from the data, implemented through the Machine Learning Engine, is available to the public in real-time. This allows participants to see in real-time the textual representation of their deliberations, how much time each participant spent talking, what are the word frequency (word clouds, n-grams and word co-occurrence) of the conversation, topic detection, point summarisation, graph representation of topics, entities relations and main points, as well as the capability to switch to a different language. Crucially, the customization capabilities are suited to the users' particular needs - whether moderators, participants, online participants, giving them an easy and personalised set of graphical interfaces, which relies on both the Data Engine and the Machine Learning Engine.

Moreover, to increase inclusiveness, the system provides a hybridization of online and offline participants - via an advanced avatar technology seek to provide bi-directional inclusiveness. Therefore, the HELIOSPHERE platform provides a spatial virtual physical concept that uses avatar technology to include large numbers of online debate participants (scale). Such capabilities become increasingly more critical in times of global pandemics, where offline gatherings of more than two people are prohibited for an extended time.

The immersive multimedia debate concept combines a look around - where all participants, local or virtual, are situated around the same round table and can be viewed by everyone in their positions rather than on opposite sides of a rectangular table - with a look inside - where AI-driven analytics support the addition and verification of insights by analysing a given pool of trustworthy media sources of multiple origins. This guarantees the real-time detection of fake assumptions and bias. The HELIOSPHERE dashboard visualises certain meta-aspects of the debate, signalling preference and contradicting opinions while they are detected. Especially in cases where debutants contradict their assumptions, this ensures participants stick to rational and honest statements and explain a possible change of opinion - after all, a difference of opinions is usually legitimate and often recommendable. Still, it should be treated openly and fairly by both speaker and listener.

With the spread of online interaction possibilities, the graphical representation of users has become ever more ubiquitous. With the origins for on-screen representation of users lying in 1980s computer games, and then spreading to personal icons in 1990s web culture, new messaging apps provide playful personalization as standard features (e.g., "Memoji/Animoji" on iOS, BitMoji on Snapchat, face filters on Instagram). Avatars offer users a sense of anonymity (they are not as recognisable as profile pictures or video chats) while retaining a sense of familiarity and personality to other participants. In a debating or conversational setting, we will use these properties of the medium to facilitate and improve online participation in physical contexts.

When avatars are displayed as audience members on screens, this brings them one step closer to the audience that can look at each other in the eye. Understandably, various modes in which online audiences can be blended in with a physical group of people - be that through 2D interfaces like monitors and screens, or 3D presences using hologram technology or robotics can be utilised to understand the most suitable solution depending on the gathering. Robotic presence is already used in classrooms worldwide to represent a teacher in the home of missing students or distant students in a school. The interaction challenge is explored to find the natural fit for engaging groups of audiences while retaining the possibility for anonymity and keeping the tone of the conversation straightforward and open.

3.3 The heliosphere visualisation engine

Finally, the visualisation engine integrates rich-media of user-generated and broadcaster provided content to empower participants to point to content (host-based, web or social media) to support or debunk arguments within a debate. Moreover, users can participate in validating if statements and content are valid and trustworthy.

To support live debates in hybrid (both online and offline) environments, HELIOSPHERE implements an immersive and interactive experience for an online debate calls for a variety of media elements such as 360° live video, Live video from remote individuals, Live generated closed captions, and automatic subtitles in different languages. This contributes to the immersive experience for Citizen participation and active contribution to a debate.

All interacting components need to be fast and synchronised so that they reach all viewers simultaneously. Since the diverse participants in the debate have differing roles and needs, these elements need to be i) object-based, ii) individually configurable, and iii) have low latency.

It is envisaged that the HELIOSPHERE provides the capability of covering debates on TV as an enhanced and interactive experience. This can be made possible via a central integration system offered by broadcasters. Moreover, data can be made available centrally and accessed directly by all interested journalists and newsrooms with just a few clicks. The use and republishing of the content are free of charge. The new content exchange platform is intended to enable citizens, and the content created is made available via diverse channels.

This can be provided as a recording or as a live debate. In this way, specific topics provided for free by the broadcasters can also be made available. For a debate to be planned, a schedule is to be developed, which allows the debate's organiser to define the services available for each debate, for example, Dashboard, 360° streaming, Link sharing for Twitter, Xing, LinkedIn, etc.

4. Initial prototype and testing of the heliosphere concept

An initial trial with a basic configuration of the HELIOSPHERE concept was carried out over two events in the Science Gallery Dublin[10], Ireland. In both cases, the HELIOSPHERE was part of the Science Gallery Book Club[11]. The first book club, which was on 26 November 2019, discussed the book 'Invisible Women: Data Bias in a World Designed for Men' by Caroline Criado Perez, and the second book club on 25 March 2020 focused on 'Clearing the Air: the Beginning and the End of Air Pollution' by Tim Smedley. It is worth pointing out that for the first book club, 'Invisible Women' HELIOSPHERE deployed a live 360 camera and language analytics features with an audience of over 20 people participating live and 15 online, for the second Bookclub 'Clearing the air' a purely online event with about 13 participants was conducted and no 360-degree camera was used. This was due to the COVID19 pandemic and allowed testing the HELIOSPHERE concept purely online and not hybrid offline and online.

To increase the inclusiveness of all attending participants, the layout was circular (see **Figure 1**). For each book club, two moderators were active, one primary and one support. During the 'Invisible Women' event, the two moderators were seated at a round table, capable of holding up to five people. Three more

[10] https://dublin.sciencegallery.com/
[11] more information can be found under http://heliosphere.social

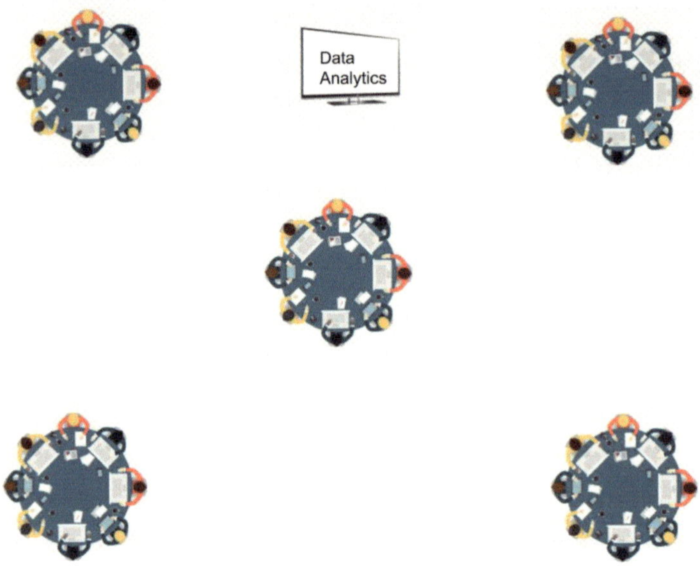

Figure 1.
HELIOSPHERE spatial concept.

tables were positioned around the table, each hosting one sub-moderator with three to five participants. For the first 40–50 minutes, the participants at each of the tables discussed the book among themselves and a designated sub-moderator. Once the initial discussion was completed, each table's sub-moderators joined the main round discussion table with the leading two moderators. Here, a 360-degree live feed camera was placed to include online viewers and participate in the debate. Their comments were relayed to the moderators via an iPad on the main table. For transparency and fairness, the HELIOSPHERE AI analytics component was enabled and displayed on a screen. A microphone in the moderation table's centre captured the discussion and encoded the audio to the AI module for further analysis. **Figure 2** depicts the view from the 360-degree camera during the live stream and debate. The table scene is the audience discussing the book with one of the moderators. The bright screen is set to showcase the debate analytics in real-time. The top left corner presents a control for the camera, so each online participant has a complete view of what is happening in real-time in the room. Additionally, the

Figure 2.
HELIOSPHERE 360 camera angle.

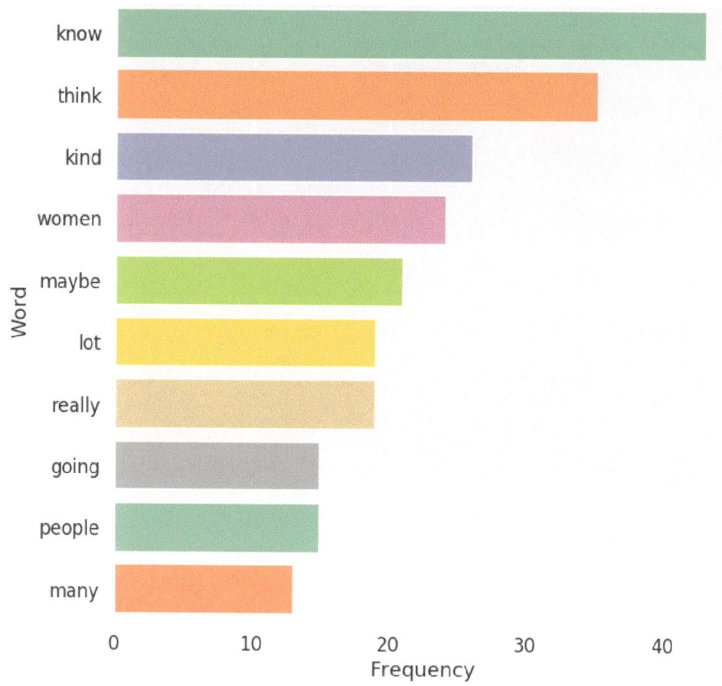

Figure 3.
Example of real-time keyword extraction.

online audience can ask questions/comments, which are then raised by the moderators and addressed during the discussion.

The AI analytics module used speech-to-text technology to encode the live voice feed in real-time, including the conversation between moderators, the author, the present and the online audience. During and after the debate, several types of analysis were performed. For transparency, the most frequently used words during the entire conversation were displayed live (see **Figures 3** and **4** as representations due to the live feed not being captured at these events for privacy reasons).

The moderators understood the general audience attitude during the debates based on real-time sentiment analysis and the emotional disposition during the debate (**Figure 5** for Invisible women discussion and **Figure 6** for Clearing the Air). In the two particular debates, the sentiment analysis for 'Invisible women' mainly was positive. Simultaneously, the topic of pollution and current societal problems emerging for the issue produces slightly more negative sentiments than the invisible women discussion.

To gain a more in-depth overview, we included a graph representation of words and topics. Each debate concept graph is connected to the overall "Heliosphere" of topics, themes, with the possibility of further analysis on the HELIOSPHERE website. Moreover, it included an n-gram analysis for both debates. This allowed us to build go-occurrence networks (graphs). For the 'Invisible Women' the words most often associated with the word "women" are indicated, which include "need", "lot", "many", "gained, "educational", "potential", "body", as well as others. For the 'Clearing the Air' discussion, the co-occurrence graph is presented in. The lower plot presents the words associated with the word "air", which include "chemica", "reaction", "pollution", "breathe", "monitor", "clear", "city", "world", "quality", among others.

The creation of n-grams serves several simultaneous purposes. First, it provides a real-time interactive concept map for users to browse and click on each node (word

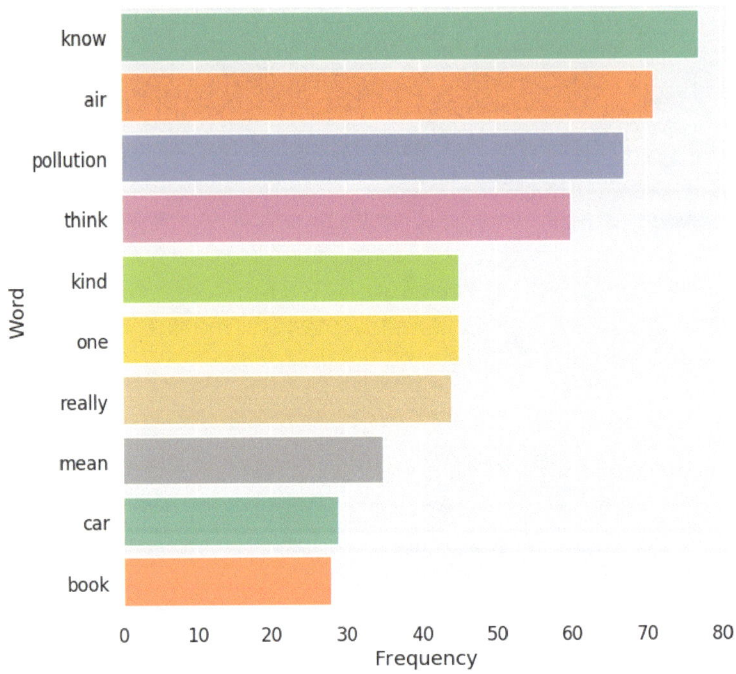

Figure 4.
Example of real-time keyword extraction.

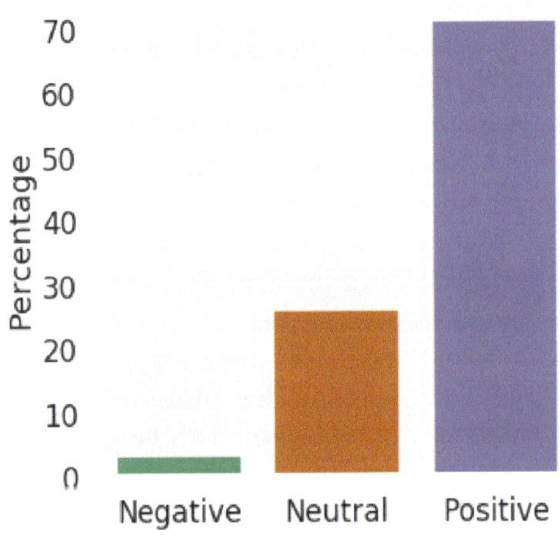

Figure 5.
Sentiment example.

or n-gram) to bring up more detailed information about the entity, concept, word. Through the concept mapping, HELIOSPHERE attempts to level the information accessible to all participants to make more informed and transparent choices/arguments. Moreover, since all participants have access to the same set of facts/data, we reduce false information while enriching the informational landscape. Technically, such information is extracted from the sources described in Section 2 of the current work. When a falsehood is present, it is labelled as such in the concept map, so users have a clear idea of the presented information's truthfulness (**Figure** 7).

Second, the n-grams provide the initial structure for the argument module, which allows us to track the participants' position on topics (whether they are for,

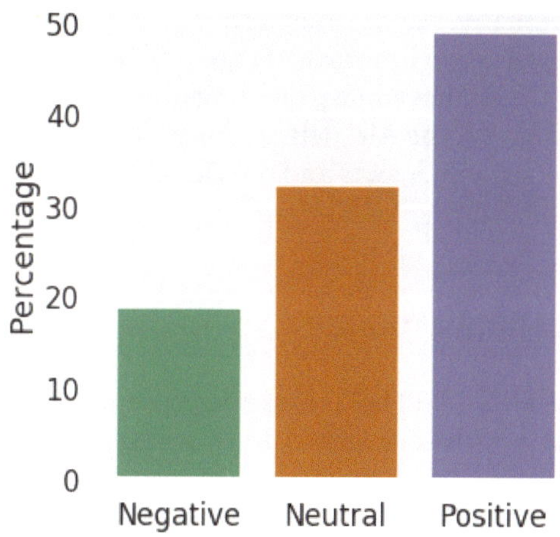

Figure 6.
Sentiment example.

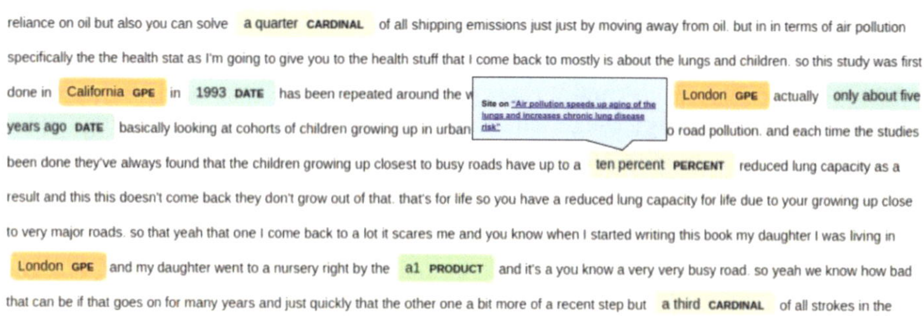

Figure 7.
Example of entity extraction.

Figure 8.
AIF argument example structure.

against or neutral). The stance tracking would be crucial during debates on essential/current social, political or economic issues. The modules serve as an indispensable tool to track the electorate's mood, thereby creating an instantaneous snapshot in the discourse. Additionally, the module connects to the AIF database through API (programmable application interface) to query AIF argument structures, enriching the debate in real-time while providing ground truth for debates. For instance, within the 'Clearing the Air' debate, the pollution due to livestock eating was debated, which the system detects and queries aid to supplement the discussion further (**Figure 8**).

5. Privacy and ethics implications

The core concept of HELIOSPHERE is to overcome the crisis of trust seeded by the use of Social Media to influence and manipulate large parts of society towards opinion forming. HELIOSPHERE, by its architecture, does not rely on storing information or using a centralised architecture to avoid similar pitfalls. The independent infrastructure via small, portable and affordable computer units described above ensures is specifically designed to provide no information needs to be stored or processed on an external server. Therefore, it can be argued that HELIOSPHERE works based on a trust-by design paradigm, which empowers real-time support from the AI approach. To increase ensure, privacy-sensitivity is provided. HELIOSPHERE does not rely on any personal information. The speech to text approach is not designed to identify specific and unique patterns over time but focuses on overall sentiment and terminology usage. There is, therefore, no temporal tracking in place that allows a comprehensive analysis of a specific individual. Ethically the concept has to evolve to 'explain' how the information has been collected and summarised. Hence, explainable AI needs to be applied to ensure ethical considerations can be taken into account, such as data decision transparency. Furthermore, it has to be assured that the approach does not evolve to 'making decisions' for both the moderator and the participants. Concepts that imply trust at its core are support mechanisms and should not undermine the moderators or participants trust in their judgement.

6. Conclusions and future work

This publication introduces and discusses the HELIOSPHERE concept. The foundations are to support the democratic process by empowering debates, both offline and online. Moreover, the HELIOSPHERE presents a hybrid image in which offline (physical) and offline are blended. To support the discussion, three main dimensions are addressed: transparency, inclusiveness, fairness. To empower openness and fairness, an AI dashboard was presented, including an initial trial. The AI dashboards support both the participants and the moderators to balance the debate based on objective data related to sentiment and most debated topics. Concerning inclusiveness state of the art camera technology such as 360-degree cameras were introduced.

Concerning future work, all three areas, transparency, inclusiveness, and fairness, are to be extended towards the vision presented in the publication's introduction. Specifically, concerning transparency and fairness, the AI dashboard is being developed and tested towards speaker time detection, speaker gender detection, off-topic detection and bias detection. More advanced technological approaches are being tested concerning inclusiveness, such as avatar technology, to overcome the barrier between online and offline audiences. For HELIOSPHERE, it is essential that not only the online audience is to be included more in the debate via camera, voice and commenting technology but also that the offline (physical) audience are more aware of the online audience, which is currently mainly an image or face on a screen. Using more advanced avatar representations makes it possible to bring the online audience closer to the experience within the space.

A further area that can be extended is to detect sentiment in debate and towards mentioned topics. This allows a moderator to 'take the heat out of a debate. On the flip side, a moderator can also be informed that the overall debate has slowed down too much and needs to be reignited. Features such as speaking time per gender and other balancing metrics are possible and can also be extended to more sophisticate areas such as bias and off-topic detection.

Finally, it has to be noted that the recent surge in sizeable real-time scale online debating platforms such as Clubhouse[12] have become very popular and has reached over 10 M active users weekly[13]. Competitors such as Twitter and Facebook are rumoured to be developing alternative real-time debating platforms with the same premisses that the conversations are not recorded or post-analysed.

In conclusion, it can be stated that the introduction of the HELIOSPHERE concept forms a solid and foundational concept to blend complex online and offline communication, such as highly interactive debates, and with that support democracy as one of the foundations of society, which is democracy.

Acknowledgements

This work is supported by the ADAPT Centre, funded under the Science Foundation Ireland Research Centres Programme (Grant 13/RC/2106).

[12] https://www.joinclubhouse.com/

[13] https://www.statista.com/statistics/1199871/number-of-clubhouse-users/

Author details

Kevin Koidl
Trinity College Dublin, Dublin, Ireland

*Address all correspondence to: kevin.koidl@scss.tcd.ie

IntechOpen

© 2021 The Author(s). Licensee IntechOpen. This chapter is distributed under the terms of the Creative Commons Attribution License (http://creativecommons.org/licenses/by/3.0), which permits unrestricted use, distribution, and reproduction in any medium, provided the original work is properly cited.

References

[1] Nabatchi T (2012) An Introduction to Deliberative Civic Engagement. In: Nabatchi T, Gastil J, Weiksner M, et al. (eds) Democracy in Motion: Evaluating the Practice and Impact of Deliberative Civic Engagement. Oxford: Oxford University Press, pp.3-39

[2] Boulianne, Shelley. "Mini-publics and public opinion: Two survey-based experiments." Political Studies 66.1 (2018): 119-136.

[3] Fung, A. (2003). Survey article: Recipes for public spheres: Eight institutional design choices and their consequences. Journal of Political Philosophy, 11(3), 338-367.

[4] Fishkin JS and Luskin RC (1999) Bringing Deliberation to the Democratic Dialogue. In: McCombs M and Reynolds A (eds) The Poll with a Human Face: The National Issues Convention Experiment in Political Communication. Mahwah, NJ: Lawrence Erlbaum, pp.3-38

[5] Gastil J, Knobloch KR and Kelly M (2012) Evaluating Deliberative Public Events and Projects. In: Nabatchi T, Gastil J, Weiksner M, et al. (eds) Democracy in Motion: Evaluating the Practice and Impact of Deliberative Civic Engagement. Oxford: Oxford University Press, pp.205-230.

[6] Grönlund K, Setälä M and Herne K (2010) Deliberation and Civic Virtue Lessons from a Citizen Deliberation Experiment. European Political Science Review 2 (1): 95-117.

[7] Holm, Søren. "A general approach to compensation for losses incurred due to public health interventions in the infectious disease context." Monash Bioethics Review (2020): 1-15.

[8] Kanra, B. (2012). Binary deliberation: The role of social learning in divided societies. Journal of Public Deliberation, 8 (1), 1.

[9] Niemeyer, S. (2011). The emancipatory effect of deliberation: Empirical lessons from mini-publics. Politicsand Society, 39(1), 103-140.

[10] Elstub, S. (2014). Mini-publics: Issues and cases. In S. Elstub & P. McLaverty (Eds.), Deliberativedemocracy: Issues and cases (pp. 166-188). Edinburgh: Edinburgh University Press.

[11] Bächtiger A, Setälä M and Grönlund K (2014) Towards a New Era of Deliberative Mini-publics. In: Grönlund K, Bächtiger A and Setälä M (eds) Deliberative Mini-publics: Involving Citizens in the Democratic Process. Colchester: European Consortium for Political Research Press, pp.225-245.

[12] Mansbridge, J., Bohman, J., Chambers, S., Christiano, T., Fung, A., Parkinson, J., & Warren, M. E. (2012). A systemic approach to deliberative democracy. In J. Parkinson & J. Mansbridge (Eds.), Deliberative systems: Deliberative democracy at the large scale (pp. 1-26). Cambridge: Cambridge University Press

[13] Curato, N., & Böker, M. (2016). Linking mini-publics to the deliberative system: A research agenda. Policy Sciences, 49(2), 173-190.

[14] Barber, B.R. (1984), Strong Democracy: Participatory Politics for a New Age, Los Angeles: University of California Press.

[15] Dahl, R.A. (1989), Demokratin och dess Antagonister [Democracy and its Critics], New Haven: Yale University Press.

[16] Davies, T. and R. Chandler (2011), 'Online deliberation design: choices,

criteria, and evidence', in T. Nabatchi, M. Weiksner, J. Gastil and M. Leighninger (eds), Democracy in Motion: Evaluating the Practice and Impact of Deliberative Civic Engagement, Oxford: Oxford University Press, pp. 103-134.

[17] Baek, Y.M., M. Wojcieszak and M.X. Delli Carpini (2011),'Online versus face-to-face deliberation: Who? Why? What? With what effects?', New Media & Society 14(3): 1-21

[18] Dahlberg, L. (2001), 'The internet and democratic discourse–exploring the prospects of online deliberativeforums extending the public sphere', Information, Communication & Society 4(4): 615-633

[19] Sunstein, Cass R. # Republic: Divided democracy in the age of social media. Princeton University Press, 2018.

[20] Pariser, Eli. The filter bubble: What the Internet is hiding from you. Penguin UK, 2011

[21] Jamieson, K. H., & Cappella, J. N. (2008). Echo chamber: Rush Limbaugh and the conservative media establishment. Oxford University Press.

[22] Benoit, W. L., Hansen, G. J., & Verser, R. M. (2003). A meta-analysis of the effects of viewing US presidential debates. Communication Monographs, 70(4), 335-350.

[23] Garrett, R. K. (2009). Echo chambers online?: Politically motivated selective exposure among Internet news users. Journal of Computer-Mediated Communication, 14(2), 265-285.

[24] Cadwalladr, C., & Graham-Harrison, E. (2018). Revealed: 50 million Facebook profiles harvested for Cambridge Analytica in major data breach. The guardian, 17, 22.

[25] Blitz, Marc Jonathan. "Lies, Line Drawing, and Deep Fake News." Okla. L. Rev. 71 (2018): 59.

[26] de Prado, Miguel, et al. "AI Pipeline-bringing AI to you. End-to-end integration of data, algorithms and deployment tools." arXiv preprint arXiv:1901.05049 (2019).

Chapter 2

From Monolithic Satellites to the Internet of Satellites Paradigm: When Space, Air, and Ground Networks Become Interconnected

Joan A. Ruiz-de-Azua, Anna Calveras and Adriano Camps

Abstract

From the first satellite launched in 1957, these systems always have drawn the attention of telecommunications operators. Thanks to their natural orbit, satellites can provide coverage to the entire globe or serve a vast region. Is this feature that makes them potential systems to extend current ground networks over the space. The first satellites were conceived as a single backhaul system to broadcast television or phone calls. Over the years, this concept evolved to a group of satellites that compose a constellation to interconnect any user around the globe. Nowadays, these constellations are still evolving to massive architectures with thousands of satellites that are interconnected between them composing satellite networks. Additionally, with the emergence of 5G, the community has started to discuss how to integrate satellites in this infrastructure. A review of the evolution of the satellites for broadband communications is presented in this chapter, discussing the novel and future proposed architectures. The presented work concludes with the potential of these satellite systems to compose a hybrid and heterogeneous architecture in which space, air, and ground networks become interconnected.

Keywords: Satellite networks, Non-Terrestrial Networks, Satellite communications, Internet of Satellites, Mega-constellations

1. Introduction

Since 1957 with the launch of the first artificial satellite *Sputnik 1*, space has been populated by a wide variety of satellite systems. The development of new technologies proliferated the emergence of different satellite platforms for multiple purposes. The global miniaturization of the technology influenced the satellite design by enabling small satellites with reduced mass. This trend not only drove the satellite shape, but also noteworthy impacted on the perception of a satellite, and its development.

This has been reflected also in satellites developed to provide broadband telecommunications services. The global coverage and large spot areas are features that naturally characterize satellites, and which telecommunications operators may leverage to deploy services. Therefore, the first satellite to provide television broadcast was launched in 1964 [1]. New missions and systems followed this launch, achieving better communications performance from space, and certifying that satellites may become a crucial system in these services [2, 3]. The achieved results encouraged to go a step forward on the design of satellite constellations. These constellations are composed of a group of satellites that work for the same goals. In this case, these constellations were conceived to provide phone services in low-orbit regions. Iridium or Globalstar are examples of the viability of the system [4, 5].

These constellations enabled to think about systems in which satellites are interconnected with Inter-Satellite Links (ISL) to exchange data [6]. These new systems represent satellite networks that dynamically change their behavior over time. With this new concept, novel architectures to optimize this dynamic behavior were presented [7–10]. From the proper definition of a single network to the integration of different constellations, each of those proposals presented unique features to enhance satellite services.

The apparition of the New Space concept and all the associated technology development also drove the novel progress in the broadband telecommunications domain [11]. In particular, the apparition of the mega-constellations became an important disruption in the concept of traditional constellations [12–14]. This architecture proposes the deployment of thousands of satellites to provide global Internet coverage. Among the different technology challenges, this approach also triggered the discussion of other difficulties related to frequency allocation or satellite manufacture procedure [15, 16]. An alternative to these massive constellations proposed the collaboration between satellites to share unused downlink opportunities. The Internet of Satellites (IoSat) paradigm [17] proposes the establishment of temporal satellite networks according to the necessity to exchange data. This dynamic environment poses new communications challenges that must be addressed in future researches.

The fifth-generation technology standard for cellular networks (5G) has been already established on the ground infrastructure as a fast, reliable, and high-connectivity communications interface for cellphones and other devices. Nevertheless, current discussions are still been performed on how to integrate satellite systems in this infrastructure [18]. Thanks to its global coverage, satellites become potential systems to expand current ground networks with a Non-Terrestrial Network (NTN) [19]. This network leverages this high altitude architecture which awards the satellites with unique qualities for the 5G. The large coverage area of spaceborne telecommunications systems enhances the service continuity in case that is not being ensured by ground infrastructure. Furthermore, satellite coverage enhances the network capacity by serving a myriad of end-users with a single spot. Finally, the orbit trajectory of a satellite allows reaching the service ubiquity on the entire globe, being able to provide services in remote and typically inaccessible areas.

This chapter surveys the evolution of satellites for broadband telecommunications services that have been experienced in the last years. Details of each developed technology are presented and discussed the implications on current and future network infrastructure. The remainder of the chapter is structured as follows. First, the apparition of broadband telecommunications satellites is presented in Section 2. Section 3 presents the satellite constellations that provided novel broadband services. The concept of satellite networks is discussed in Section 4. The impact of the New Space trend is presented in Section 5. Section 6 presents the novel concept of IoSat, while Section 7 discusses the integration of satellites in the 5G infrastructure. Finally, Section 8 concludes the chapter.

2. The apparition of communications satellites

Satellites have always been bounded to broadband telecommunications thanks to their large visibility of the Earth. This capability is inherited from their natural movement. Satellites are celestial bodies which constantly move tracing an elliptical trajectory around another larger celestial body. The broadband telecommunications satellites orbit around the Earth. This distinctive motion is defined by means of the Keplerian orbital parameters or elements. These six parameters determine the shape and size of the ellipse, the orientation of the orbital plane with respect to the Earth, the orientation of the ellipse in this plane, and the location of the satellite along this trajectory.

Satellite orbits are gravitationally curved trajectories which can be represented in a two-dimensional trajectory located in a plane. This plane is known as orbital plane, and two Keplerian elements determine its orientation with respect to the Earth: (1) the longitude of the ascending node (Ω) corresponds to the horizontal angle between the plane and the origin of the longitudes (the Greenwich meridian or prime meridian); (2) the inclination angle (i) determines the vertical orientation of the plane with respect to the origin of the latitudes (the equator). The orbit shape traced in this plane is determined by (3) the semi-major axis (a) that corresponds to half the distance between the periapsis and apoapsis of the orbit, and (4) the eccentricity (e) which describes how much the ellipse is elongated compared to a circle. The resulting ellipse can be rotated in the same plane determined by (5) the angle known as argument of periapsis (ω). A satellite travels this elliptical curve over time, moving periodically among numerous locations. The position of a satellite in this ellipse is represented by the (6) the true anomaly (ν) which corresponds to the angle of the satellite location at a specific epoch or time with respect to the direction of the periapsis.

The ensemble of Keplerian elements allow the characterization of the satellite position, and its complete trajectory. **Figure 1** represents these parameters to clarify their meaning.

Numerous orbits exist depending on the values of the Keplerian elements, which laid the foundation of different classifications. Among them, the classification based on satellite altitude prevails, which determines implicitly the orbit semi-major axis. In this classification, satellite orbit are structured in three main blocks: (1) Low Earth Orbits (LEO) are identified by altitude values between 200 km and 2000 km; (2) Medium Earth Orbits (MEO) correspond to those orbits with an altitude encompassed between 2000 km and 35,786 km; Finally, (3) Geosynchronous Equatorial Obrits (GEO), also known as geostationary orbits, are determined by a specific altitude of 35,786 km. Is in this last type of orbit, indeed, in which

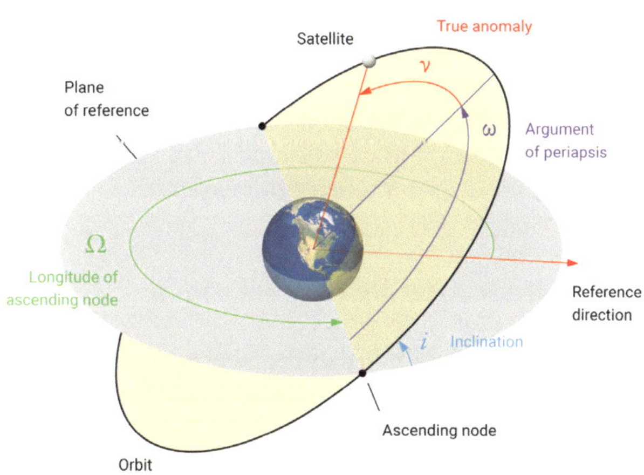

Figure 1.
Representation of the Keplerian elements that represents the orbit trajectory of a satellite (gray sphere), and its plane (yellow surface) with respect to the equatorial plane (gray surface).

telecommunications operators identified potential characteristics to deploy satellites that broadcast multiple services.

Satellites that orbit following GEO trajectories are characterized to be deployed in an orbit plane located at the equator of the Earth, and following a circular orbit (i.e. inclination 0° and eccentricity 0). This combination of inclination, eccentricity and altitude allows a satellite to constantly move at the same velocity than the Earth rotation. Therefore, a GEO satellite constantly observes the same region of the Earth, and remains them as fixed points in the sky. These characteristics are ideal to provide broadband services for specific geo-political regions, such as television delivery, military applications, or generic telecommunications.

Since the launch of the Syncom 3 satellite at 1964 [1], geostationary large-satellites became the standard configuration to provide these services. This was the first GEO satellite deployed to provide television coverage of the Summer Olympics. Its launches promoted the apparition of other GEO satellites, such as the Intelsat I (nickname Early Bird) satellite at 1965. In paritcular, this satellite was developed by the company Intelsat to demonstrate that communications through this kind of orbit were feasible. It was used during four years and four months to provide multiple services among different missions, standing out the first live television coverage and its participation in the Apollo 11 mission.

This satellite was the first one to provide direct communications contact between Europe and North America, handling telephone, television, and telefacsimile transmissions. This satellite paved the way to develop such kind of backhaul systems to communicate around the glove, and it was the first of a large family of Intelsat satellite that reaches current epoch with Intelsat 39 launched in 2019.

Over the different missions, the developments on these satellites have been focused on the optimization and adjustment of the Internet mechanisms, techniques, and protocols to enhance the throughput over satellites. With the advent of the different versions of the Digital Video Broadcast - Satellite (DVB-S) protocols [2], the television broadcast over satellites was also investigated as part of the digitalization of this service. The outcome of all these efforts was the development of the high throughput satellites, so-called next-generation satellites [3].

These GEO satellites has coped the broadband telecommunications activity during the last years with the mission development from companies like Hughes Space and Communications, Space Systems/Loral (SSL), Orbital Science Corporation, Lockheed Martin, Thales Alenia Space, and Airbus-Astrium. They are currently part of our space environment, and keep providing telecommunication service to interconnect fixed regions in the globe. This interconnection is also characterized by having a considerable delay transmission, around 900 ms (approximatelly). Although its static relative position becomes ideal for coverage region, this large delay values may not be suitable for services deployed in the Internet. Therefore, new approaches emerged to compensate this long delay with lower-altitude regions, and to integrate Internet services in these satellite systems.

3. The era of low-altitude satellite constellations

Gaffney et al. analyzed the feasibility of the new non-geosynchronous or non-geostationary satellite systems proposed on the US Federal Communications Commission (FCC) by different private companies [20]. These innovative proposals enhanced the communications end-to-end latency using MEO, and LEO satellites. Those orbit regions were not originally proposed because of the continuous relative movement—unlike the geosynchronous case—that satellite experience. Satellites in this configuration suffer from a small field of view and temporal contact with ground devices, which leads to service disruptions. Therefore, satellite constellations have risen as a promising architecture to deal with this challenge, by performing user handovers between adjacent satellites. An in-depth study of the benefits of applying these constellations was presented in the dissertation [21]. Kashitani remarks that satellite constellations at LEO region can serve a larger number of customers with a relatively reduced deployment cost as compared to their MEO homonyms.

These performance expectations encouraged the development of numerous LEO satellite constellations by private companies. Globalstar emerged as a private company that could provide satellite phone and low-speed data communications with a dedicated satellite constellation [5]. The first satellites were launched in 1998 to start composing a constellation that would be finished in 2000. The Globalstar constellation was composed of satellites that worked as bent pipes or repeaters between two users located in the same spot. Although this design enables remote users to communicate, the system was also limited by having a common satellite to interconnect the end devices. If this common satellite was not available, the communication was not feasible.

The Orbcomm company developed a specific constellation to deal with this situation offering discontinuous coverage between end-users. Unlike the previous case, this constellation was designed to provide low-speed data communications, and it was not capable to offer telephone services. To provide this discontinuous coverage, satellites in this constellation were able to store incoming messages to download them later over another region. This store-and-forward mechanism was crucial to achieve this desired performance and became a key technology to develop the concept of Disruption Tolerant Networks (presented in the following section).

Alternatively to the previous constellations, Iridium Communications company decided to deploy its constellation to provide voice and data coverage to custom satellite phones [4]. This new constellation, known as Iridium, extended the original concept by interconnecting satellites with radio interfaces to relay data down to the ground; i.e. the development of Inter-Satellite Links (ISL). By defining a custom and specific constellation, a route between two end-users and composed of satellites could be defined. This revolutionized the concept of satellite constellation because they could transfer data among the satellites with a reduced delay. The original Iridium constellation was extended with a new generation of 66 satellites, called Iridium NEXT, in 2017. This extension aimed to enhance the satellite capacity from 2.4 kbps to 1.5 Mbps, using high-throughput techniques.

The LEO satellite constellations proposed for broadband telecommunications revolutionized the concept by evolving from a repeater-based approach for voice and data, passing through a store-and-forward solution for data, and reaching an interconnected architecture for voice and data. This last approach presented a constellation as a set of satellites that compose a network. This new satellite network concept paved the way for new interconnected architectures.

4. Interconnecting satellites to compose satellite networks

This ISL concept revolutionized the perception of satellite constellations, which started to be conceived as networks composed of satellites. Werner discusses the challenges of deploying these networks and concludes that satellite mobility is a key factor in the stability of the links that compose the network [7]. In particular, the nature of an ISL is determined by the relative motion between two satellites. Therefore, an ISL may be feasible and active during a lapse of time depending on the orbits.

These temporal links are also known as satellite contacts and drive the topology representation of a satellite network. In particular, a topology is represented by a set of nodes that are interconnected by edges. Werner proposed the representation of a satellite network topology with the concept of a snapshot. A snapshot of a network is the topology representation with the connections established between the satellites that remain stable during a lapse of time. The creation or destruction of an ISL results in the generation of another snapshot. The overall generated snapshots compose a sequence that represents the evolution of the topology over time.

Figure 2 presents an example with three snapshots, identified by s_k (s_0, s_1 and s_2), that remain stables between the lapse of times t_i (snapshot s_0 remains stable between t_0 and t_1). This evolution is characterized by the movement of the nodes, which in this case corresponds to the orbit trajectory. Therefore, the number of snapshots and its stability time depends directly on satellite orbits and their communications means. Just as a brief reminder, this motion is determined by a set of parameters that allow estimating the complete trajectory of a satellite. Furthermore, this trajectory follows a periodic pattern, if no orbit disturbances are considered. Consequently, the sequence of snapshots is periodic and predictable.

The transition of these snapshots may represent an evolution of a satellite network in which parts of it are isolated during a lapse of time. These isolated fragments of the network may be sporadically connected with other satellites over time, depending on the nature of satellite contacts. This intermittent connectivity encourages to define an environment in which network partitions are frequent, and satellites must leverage opportunistic and sporadic satellite contacts to communicate. The understanding of this temporal nature of satellite contacts becomes crucial in the definition of end-to-end routes in this scenario.

Delay and Disruption Tolerant Networks (DTN) approaches envision the establishment of routes in this disruptive environment [9]. A proposal to solve this disruption is a store-and-forward approach, that is a way to store messages from a satellite to lately propagate them to another satellite was conceived to leverage the opportunistic and sporadic satellite contacts. Nevertheless, the definition mechanisms to identify end-to-end routes in this disruptive environment were largely discussed.

Among the different proposed techniques, a classification was conducted in [22] based on the generation of replicas of the messages. In this regard, a protocol that replicates messages is known as a replication-based protocol, which is characterized by delivering the data to the destination according to a probability, based on the number of replicas generated. Alternatively, a forwarding-based protocol estimates future satellite contacts to define routes over time, requiring a larger computational effort. Authors in [22] conclude that it must exist a balance between future knowledge of the network evolution, and the computational capacity.

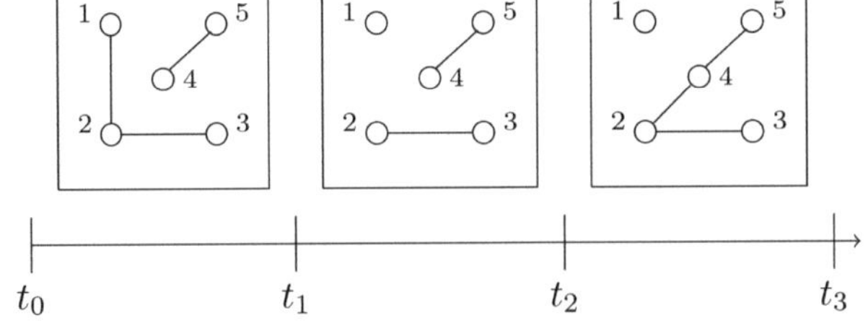

Figure 2.
Representation of different snapshots (s_k) over time (t_i) associated with five satellites. Figure from [17].

The Iridium constellation aimed to compensate this topology evolution and mitigate network disruption by conceiving a custom constellation architecture that would later be known as LEO Satellite Networks. Ekici et al. started to work with a satellite constellation configuration that mitigates this mobility impact on the communications performance [6].

The constellation is designed with an orchestrated and fixed architecture in which satellites are specifically located on purpose. This constellation builds a mesh architecture in which each satellite has four satellite-to-satellite interfaces to communicate with its neighbors. The resulting topology of the network is characterized by nodes located in a grid with a set of rows and columns. Despite this design to mitigate the disruption, satellites are always in motion. However, the movement of the satellites in this constellation results in a continuous shift of the satellites in the column axis of the mesh.

This coordinated movement ensures that from the local view of a satellite the connections with its neighbors remain unaltered. This condition is satisfied in the most populated latitudes because when the satellites pass over the polar region the formation cannot be respected. Moreover, an abstract line represents a seam in this mesh that separates the direction of the satellites. On one side of this seam, the satellites move from the South to the North, while on the other side they travel in the opposite direction. Traditionally, communications through this seam were forbidden.

Figure 3 presents this satellite constellation with its corresponding mesh topology.

This constellation is founded over two classes of ISL, defined according to the vicinity of the neighbor. The intra-plane ISL allows a satellite to communicate with its two neighbors that are located in the same orbit plane. Meanwhile, the inter-plane ISL allows a satellite to communicate with its two neighbors located in adjacent planes. This differentiation was conducted because the nature of both ISL types differs: intra-plane ISL are always stable and feasible, while inter-plane ISL may be disconnected in the polar region. The goal to relay data from ground users was satisfied by defining the concept of a virtual node. This kind of node is associated with a logical location that corresponds to a square of an entire grid that covers the entire Earth surface. Each satellite is then associated with a logical location when it passes over this surface square, being responsible to serve the users allocated in this area. Due to the satellite movement, the satellite changes over time their logical

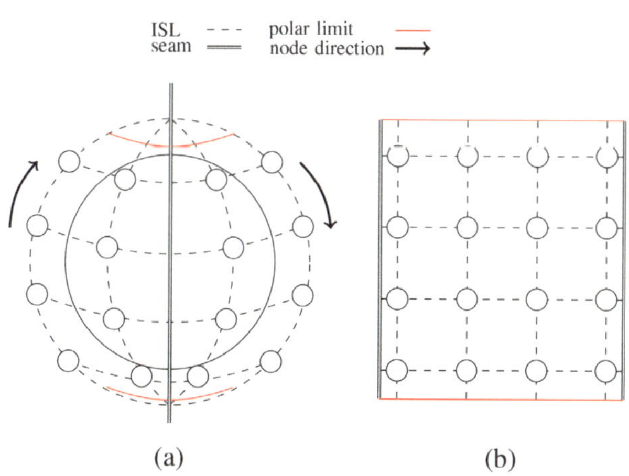

Figure 3.
Representation of (a) the constellation design that represents a LEO satellite network, and (b) its resulting map to a mesh topology. Figure from [17].

location when they bypass the corresponding square. Furthermore, the logical location is also mapped in the mesh topology by vertical and horizontal coordinates that correspond to the column and row numbers.

The LEO Satellite Network concept was extended in future researches by integrating other satellites in further orbit regions. The combination of multiple satellite systems stood out as a potential architecture to offer new capabilities or improve the capacity achieved by their own.

Multi-Layered Satellite Networks (MLSN) are a system-of-systems architecture [23] compounded of distinct satellite constellations deployed at different altitudes, which corresponds to the layers in this system. This architecture was proposed in [8] to enhance the traffic capacity and the stability of a satellite network. The proposal leverages the visibility of the satellites located at higher altitudes that can orchestrate a group of satellites deployed in lower altitudes.

A hierarchical structure in which successively upper layers always gather lower layers is designed under the previous premise. Despite the original proposal did not specifically define the type and the number of layers, the LEO, MEO, and GEO were typically the three main layers associated with this network. In this configuration, GEO satellites would manage a group of MEO satellites, which at the same time each one would gather an ensemble of LEO satellites. Satellites located in the same layer can communicate among them using Intra-Orbital Links (IOL), while they are also able to interact with satellites in adjacent layers using ISL.

Figure 4 illustrates this multi-layered architecture with the three main altitudes.

This hierarchical architecture enhances the stability of the network thanks to the large visibility of upper-layer satellites. Despite the connections between the satellites still changes over time, the topology changes correspond to fluctuations of the low-layer satellites that belong to the group of an upper-layer satellite. This feature mitigates the influence of satellite mobility on network dynamism. Nevertheless, the architecture design of the low-layer satellite system may still provoke irregular changes in the topology. [24] discussed this behavior and suggested the use of a LEO satellite network—which ensures the mesh formation—as a lowest-layer

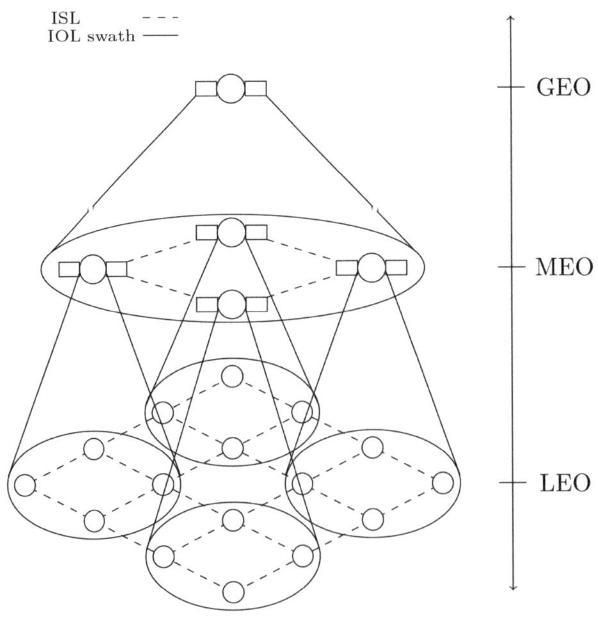

Figure 4.
Illustration of a MLSN with three layer. Figure from [17].

satellite system. This satellite constellation simplifies the computation of end-to-end routes among the layers, and in the same layer. The integration of a LEO satellite network into the MLSN demonstrates the potential of this heterogeneous architecture, that may accept including multiple distinct satellite systems.

The architectures of these satellite networks were presented considering always the traditional concept of satellite missions, in which a constellation is properly defined. Nevertheless, the apparition of new trends in the space related to the New Space movement has motivated novel concepts of satellite networks with non-conventional strategies.

5. The disruption of New Space in broadband telecommunications

Nowadays, the New Space concept is becoming an important trend that different countries leverage to encourage and promote space activities in their society. Due to the large number of new concepts associated with this movement, it is difficult to properly define the New Space trend. Authors in [11] try to clarify this concept by performing a survey of different researches. Their study concludes that this new trend is characterized by a set of key traits: (1) the apparition of new private entities that deploy novel satellite architectures in front of the traditional national space agencies; (2) novel development procedures that simplify and reduce the cost of the manufacturing of space products; and (3) the technology development is performed to always satisfy customer needs. These traits are associated with research of novel technologies related to satellite autonomy, miniaturization, satellite platforms, and crowd.

This current technological landscape would not be possible without the emergence of the CubeSat platforms [25]. This well-founded architecture was conceived in 1999 by professors Jordi Puig-Suari from California Polytechnic State University, and Bob Twiggs from Stanford University. The goal to develop a spacecraft architecture that would facilitate academic developments surprisingly triggered the creation of a new philosophy to develop satellites: the use of Commercial Off-The-Shelf (COTS) components, and the reduction of satellite dimensions. These small satellites are equipped with all the subsystems of a traditional satellite, which are composed of COTS components. This strategy speeds up spacecraft development, and drastically reduces the cost of its production. Therefore, the CubeSats are ideal platforms to investigate and develop new technologies.

The inventiveness experienced with CubeSats influenced also the traditional big-satellite activities. New private and adventurous proposals have proliferated in the last years encouraged by their commercial prospects. The most distinguished innovative application for this big platform is the deployment of satellite constellations that provide continuous Internet access. Despite the numerous improvements in the ground facilities, satellite platforms stood out as a potential system to achieve this requirement. LEO satellite constellations are naturally characterized by providing global coverage to the entire planet. Iridium constellation is an illustrative example of how this architecture can provide data access to a widespread group of ground users. Despite this infrastructure, current Iridium services are limited to a poor messages exchange (hundreds of kbps), which may not be sufficient for current and upcoming Internet services (e.g. video streaming, cloud computing, etc.) Therefore, an extension of these traditional LEO satellite constellations has been proposed to cope with this new demand.

Private companies have taken a step forward in the development of massive satellite constellations, which assemble hundreds or thousands of satellites to provide global and seamless Internet coverage with competitive interfaces; i.e. with low latency and high throughput. These ambitious goals cannot be achieved with traditional architectures nor delay-tolerant solutions.

Among the different companies, OneWeb Ltd.—previously named WorldVu—was the first one that announced the development of this macro architecture [12]. Joining efforts with Virgin Group and Qualcomm, OneWeb expected to deploy 720 satellites at 1200 km height. This LEO satellite constellation was not designed to include satellite-to-satellite architecture, which requires the deployment of further satellites to satisfy current demand [26].

Space Exploration Technologies Corp. (SpaceX) publicly announced the development of the Starlink mega-constellation one year later [13]. Starlink comprises 4425 satellites that would be distributed across several sets of orbits. Three different layers are distinguished: the main layer at 1150 km, the secondary layer at 1110 km, and the third layer at 1130 km. This macro satellite system corresponds to an MLSN thanks to the use of satellite-to-satellite laser interfaces, although all the layers are located in the LEO region. SpaceX has already deployed 1,015 satellites of its StarLink mega-constellation, having 951 still in orbit [27].

More recently, Telesat Canada envisioned deploying a massive satellite constellation of 117 small-satellites to compete with the previous constellations [14]. These satellites would include a dedicated ISL with high transmission capacity.

Preliminary studies demonstrated that these massive satellite constellations can provide communications interfaces that can satisfy high-data volumes (up to Tbps), and low-latency communications [26]. Despite the potential performance of this architecture, its enormous size poses numerous challenges. Among the different ones that have been discussed during the last years [28], six challenges stand out: (1) The required funds to maintain the development of the entire project [29]; (2) The necessity to develop and construct a satellite manufacturing infrastructure to reduce the production cost [30]; (3) the increase of space debris due to the overpopulation of the space [15]; (4) the hoarding of frequency bands due to the necessary wide bands allocations; (5) the complex administrative registry of this large number of satellites [16]; (6) Impact on other space fields, like astronomy [31] forcing to develop custom mitigation technologies [32]. These constraints make that the deployment of this massive satellite constellation feasible to specific companies or entities. Another perspective in which does not require the launch of massive constellations from independent entities needs to be conceived to balance these problems.

6. The internet of satellites paradigm

Alternatively to these massive satellite constellations, a collaborative and distributed approach has been proposed in the last years. The concept of Federated Satellite Systems (FSS) was presented by Prof. Golkar in [10]. This new satellite system essentially consists of spacecraft networks in which satellites trade unused or inefficiently allocated resources commodities, such as data storage, data processing, downlink capacity, power supply, or instrument time. This concept is analogous to terrestrial applications, such as peer-to-peer file sharing, cloud computing, and electrical power grids. In this way, FSS tried to avoid the underutilization of expensive space assets in already existing missions. The establishment of cooperation frames beyond the common mission interactions based on ground post-processing and merging of instrument data becomes more and more a necessity. Distinct-stakeholder satellite missions would leverage the establishment of in-orbit collaborations by improving current system performance or by achieving new goals.

The terminology presented in [10] allows understanding the nature of these collaborations. A *satellite federation* is composed of a group of satellites which decide to engage in a collaboration with each other during their mission. These federations allow the satellites to share or trade available *resources* which are the tangible and intangible assets that a spacecraft has (e.g. propellant, power, data processing, downlink capacity, etc.) Although the original definition encompasses generic assets, the later work investigated federations with data-centered resources, such as processing, downlink, and storage capacity.

The establishment of a satellite federation has a decision-making component—not necessarily autonomous—with which a satellite *opportunistically* deems if the collaboration is beneficial, where the benefit is defined as either economic profit or generic value. Despite the opportunity refers to the federation profit, a temporal aspect also is integrated with these characteristics. Due to the mission lifecycle of a satellite, resources are not constantly available, enabling temporal windows of opportunity in which they can be traded. During this transaction, the satellite that supplies the corresponding resources are defined as satellite *suppliers* or *providers*. When instead a satellite is seeking to request the resources, it plays the role of a *customer* in the federation. These roles may be switched over satellite lifetime depending on their interest, being also possible that a satellite acts as both customer and supplier at the same time. In the end, the joint set of customers and suppliers makes a satellite federation.

The FSS concept also differs from the other approaches, because they can be conceived as virtual satellite systems. These systems represent a group of satellites that are part of a distinct physical system–like a constellation–and they decide to create a new one that is fictitious. Traditional applications offered to ground users can be achieved with these systems, but new ones proliferate with this virtual group of satellites. Machine-to-machine applications may be deployed among the different satellites that conform the virtual system, like trajectory applications (e.g. flight formation, collision avoidance), applications that require data fusion (e.g. cloud detection, different instruments), among others. In terms of communications, this can be represented as an autonomous satellite application that deploys some services through and for satellites. All these characteristics require solutions that are flexible, adaptable, and scalable that must be reflected in all the development levels, included in the inter-satellite communications ones.

For this reason, our work in the last years has been focused on conceiving and developing the Internet of Satellites (IoSat) paradigm [17]. This approach proposes an interconnected space segment that follows these premises from satellite federations. A custom satellite infrastructure that corresponds to a network backbone is not proposed in this paradigm. Instead, it promotes the establishment of networks using peer-to-peer architectures, in which interested satellites are part of the network. The IoSat paradigm cannot be understood without firstly observe the nature of satellite federations.

FSS encourage the establishment of sporadic and opportunistic collaborations to share unallocated resources among heterogeneous satellites. It is important to understand concept-by-concept what this statement means.

The **sporadic** term refers to the possibility to deploy this collaboration at any moment. This feature makes satellite federations unpredictable events that may occur without notice, and they cannot–normally–be estimated in advance. Despite this randomness, the need to deploy federations is related to the satellite resources and the potential benefit that a satellite can award.

This is related to the **opportunistic** term, which suggests that federations are only established if related satellites envision to garner some benefits (e.g. enhancement of mission performance, an extension of satellite capabilities, payment for resources shared). This opportunism also refers to the mandatory non-degradation of the original mission. Satellites that establish a federation are designed to perform a specific mission (e.g. observation of the soil moisture, relay data from ground terminals, observe the galaxy), which must remain as its main priority. Therefore, the federation cannot degrade the performance of this mission by the undesired depletion or allocation of resources.

If the satellite does not identify a potential benefit, it must be able to **decide** not establishing a federation. This decision-making capacity becomes crucial to deploy federations and entails the awarding of a certain level of autonomy to the satellites. Finally, the satellites that collaborate are equipped with different resources and capacities.

This **heterogeneous** configuration poses multiple challenges related to resource sharing, connectivity, among others.

Following these features, the paradigm suggests dynamic, sporadic, and opportunistic satellite networks that are temporally established depending on the necessity and choice to deploy federations. These temporal networks have been called Inter-Satellite Networks (ISN) following the traditional nomenclature originated in [33]. This kind of network is created by the decision to collaborate–not necessarily for free–of satellites, that become the intermediate nodes of the network. In particular, the creation of an ISN is achieved thanks to the combination of point-to-point federations among intermediate nodes that share the possibility to communicate. **Figure 5** illustrates the paradigm philosophy by showing three ISNs (ISN_1, ISN_2, and ISN_3) which coexist simultaneously. These ISNs are created depending on the FSS requirements and they adapt themselves to manage network dynamism. Note also that some nodes can participate in multiple ISNs at the same time.

A satellite federation is established only when the transaction is required, after that the federation is no longer needed. This temporality is also reflected in the definition ISN. This corresponds that ISNs have three phases that characterize their lifetime: (1) the establishment phase, (2) the maintenance phase, and (3) the destruction phase.

The establishment of an ISN is the negotiation process in which intermediate federations are created to configure the network. During this phase, its members can decide to not accept this interaction due to their state or strategy interests. Moreover, the establishment phase ensures that the ISN can satisfy FSS requirements by providing the required services. For instance, if a security level is required, intermediate nodes should have secure mechanisms to provide it. This implies that during the ISN establishment, nodes shall indicate which services they can provide.

Once the ISN is established, the maintenance phase ensures that the network adapts to different events. In particular, as a satellite network is a dynamic

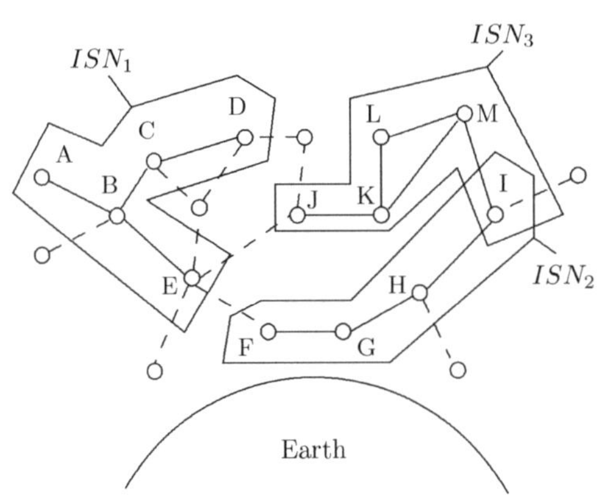

Figure 5.
IoSat space segment representation. Figure from [17].

environment in which nodes are in constant movement, this phase is responsible to update network connections when intermediate links are broken. Therefore, it should be able to replace old intermediate nodes by adding new ones. Moreover, some satellites could request to participate in an existing federation that would need to add more intermediate nodes to increase the current ISN. Thus, the ISN should be able to adhere new satellite nodes as per their request, or by the need to keep the topology stable.

Finally, in the destruction phase (once the ISN is no longer required) all the nodes that have participated in the network should perform the destruction process which cleans their internal state and recovers their usual activity. This is an important phase because the resources shall be released when they are no more needed.

There is a common need that should be respected in an ISN. Satellites are embedded systems with severe limitations in terms of energy, computation, and data storage resources, which means that additional inter-satellite communications capabilities could jeopardize the mission. This could appear because satellites are normally conceived to accomplish a specific mission, and the integration of these new capabilities could suppose an additional resource consumption that could deplete the satellite. In other words, the deployment of an ISN shall not impact the mission of intermediate satellites. Therefore, this network is deployed using a resource-aware strategy while trying to satisfy application requirements. Moreover, if a satellite decides that its participation in the network compromises the accomplishment of its mission, it can decide to leave the network. Therefore, satellites require a certain level of intelligence to autonomously take this decision. An ISN is a completely dynamic and constantly changing scenario, due to satellite mobility, node participation, and node resource state.

Our previous researches have addressed the multiple technology challenges associated with the IoSat paradigm. A predictive algorithm was developed in [34] to provide autonomous capabilities to satellites. In particular, this algorithm can estimate future satellite contacts and predict routes overtime in which federations can be established. Moreover, new protocols regarding the necessity to notify resources available (e.g. downlink opportunities) and the procedure to establish a federation were published in [35, 36]. These two protocols have been evaluated in an scenario with Earth Observation (EO) satellites that uses federations with a mega-constellation to download data. **Figure 6** presents the achieved results of these simulation, being able to duplicate the amount of bytes downloaded per day when

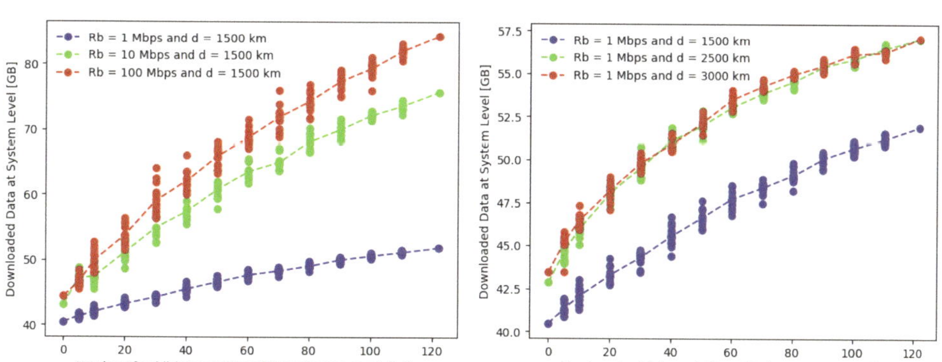

(a) with different ISL data rates (b) with different ISL maximum ranges

Figure 6.
Downloaded data of saturated EO satellites per day according to the publisher satellites and ISL subsystems with differnet maximum range (left figure) and data rates d_{max} and different data rates Rb (right figure). Figure from [35].

more satellites of the mega-constellation participates as providers of the downlink service.

Apart from these innovations, the paradigm still poses considerable challenges that must be tackled in future researches.

7. The emergence of 5G in satellite systems

The fifth-generation technology standard for cellular networks (5G) has been already established on the ground infrastructure as a fast, reliable, and high-connectivity communications interface for cellphones and other devices. The 3rd Generation Partnership Project (3GPP) developed multiple specifications that conform this standard over the years [37] to satisfy the requirements of future use-cases. These requirements were presented by the International Telecommunication Union Radiocommunication (ITU-R) sector in the International Mobile Telecommunications (IMT) for 2020 and beyond [38]. The standard presents three use-cases according to the current and future telecommunications activity: the enhanced Mobile Broadband (eMBB), the massive Machine Type Communications (mMTC), and the Ultra Reliable Low Latency Communications (URLLC). The eMBB scenario is an evolution of the mobile broadband applications developed in the previous generation standard (4G) by improving the data transfer performance and increasing the seamless experience. Both URLLC and mMTC are new use-cases that were defined due to the emergence of the Internet of Things (IoT) and the apparition of Critical Communications (CC). The IoT paradigm [39] promotes the interconnection of multiple devices that can exchange data without requiring human interaction. In this way, the mMTC represents this trend which is characterized by a myriad of connected devices that typically transmit a relatively low volume of delay-tolerant data. The URLLC scenario is centered on safety and critical applications that require real-time and reliable communications, such as control of industrial manufacturing, remote medical surgery, autonomous driving, and other emergency applications.

The 5G specifications were developed to satisfy the requirements published by the ITU-R in [40]. This development has been conducted to achieve three main goals:

- Provide high data speeds — efforts were focused to conceive new transmission techniques that satisfy the necessity of high data rates of the eMBB use-case. Therefore, enhanced downlink and uplink communications would provide data rates up to 20 Gbps and 10 Gbps respectively, ensuring hundreds of Mbps on average.

- Reduce the end-to-end latency — the URLLC applications require the data delivery process to be more instantaneous because critical services cannot suffer from delay. Therefore, the enhancements would allow reaching real-time access with end-to-end latency of less than 1 ms.

- Ensure seamless and global connectivity — the emergence of autonomous and mobile devices encourages the development of an infrastructure that enhances the continuous connection with the network. Services deployed over this network would not suffer any disruption which could compromise the performance in mMTC, eMBB, and URLLC scenarios.

Is in this last goal in which satellites have stood out as a promising platform to be integrated with the 5G infrastructure. In March 2017, 3GPP started new activities to study the role of the satellites in the 5G [19]. The outcome of these studies was the definition of the Non-Terrestrial Networks (NTN) which encompasses the multiple systems not located on the ground, such as satellites, Unmanned Aerial Vehicles (UAV), or High Altitude Platforms (HAP). This network leverages this high altitude architecture which awards the satellites with unique qualities for the 5G. In this way, the NTN are conceived following the multi-layered satellite network premise, but including in the architecture other systems than only satellites. The large coverage area of spaceborne telecommunications systems enhances the service continuity in case that is not being ensured by ground infrastructure. Furthermore, satellite coverage enhances the network capacity by serving a myriad of end-users with a single spot. Finally, the orbit trajectory of a satellite allows reaching the service ubiquity on the entire globe, being able to provide services in remote and typically inaccessible areas.

These qualities have led to the definition of multiple satellite applications in the eMBB, mMTC, and URLLC scenarios [18]. The eMBB scenario would leverage on satellite systems working as complementary traffic backhauling nodes of the network, or by reducing the handovers of those mobile nodes that perform large trajectories, such as trains or airplanes [41]. Satellites could enhance the services in the mMTC scenario depending on the area in which the devices are deployed. For wide-area services, the satellites play the important role of large visibility to become a central node that feeds device traffic. Otherwise, in local area services, the satellites become a complementary infrastructure to backhaul the traffic of a massive number of devices, like the eMBB case. Unlike the other cases, satellite altitude prevents from achieving the required end-to-end latency for URLLC cases. Nevertheless, the satellites enhance these services by providing a supporting role that broadcasts information over a wide area.

Novel private entities have observed this potential capacity of satellites to support the current 5G and IoT infrastructure, and they started the development of their satellite constellations. Lacuna Space started the development and launch of a dedicated CubeSat constellation for supporting IoT services from space [42]. Currently, they have just launched the third satellite of the constellation which uses Long Range (LoRa) communications technology. Other companies like Sateliot, Kepler Communications, or Eutelsat have also pronounced to deploy their constellations. It seems that another space race started to integrate satellites into the IoT paradigm.

8. Conclusions and way forward

During the last decades, space has been populated by a wide variety of satellite systems. From monolithic GEO satellites to current constellation approaches, space missions have experienced a considerable evolution to provide new services to the users. The traditional television broadcast and phone calls lead to more resource-demanding services based on current Internet applications. Constellations of LEO satellites have emerged as the necessary infrastructure to support these new services in space.

These constellations were originally conceived as independent satellites orbiting in an ad-hoc architecture. Nevertheless, they started to be considered as satellite networks when interactions between satellites were needed to satisfy the novel delay and throughput demands. The configuration of these interconnected satellites promoted the proliferation of different architectures to leverage on satellite altitudes or to mitigate satellite dynamics (e.g. MLSN, LEO Satellite Networks, etc.) All of them inspired satellite architectures that are currently working in space, such as

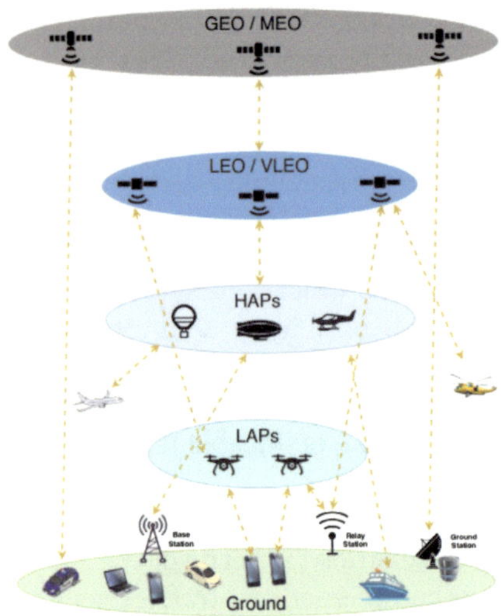

Figure 7.
NTN architecture proposed in the 3GPP. Figure from [18].

the Tracking Data Relay Satellite System (TDRSS) or the Iridium constellation [4]. In this way, the New Space trend promoted the apparition of novel flexible and distributed architectures to keep evolving the space for future user demands, like the mega-constellations or the IoSat paradigm.

The next step of this space evolution seems to be associated with the ground network revolution experienced with the 5G. The possibility to extend the current infrastructure with seamless connectivity puts satellites as potential systems for this purpose. The existence of different entities that are working on standardize the integration of satellites with ground networks, conforming the NTN concept, is an example of how satellites will become more and more a reality in our infrastructure. **Figure 7** presents a conceptual view of the NTN architecture composed of satellites, High Altitude Platforms (HAP), and Low Altitude Platforms (LAP). Different missions have started to experiment with satellite capabilities to provide IoT connection around the Earth glove. Their success demonstrates the potential of these new systems (for ground networks) and helps to believe in a promising future with heterogeneous networks composed of space, air, and ground infrastructure. Only time will tell whether this paradigm would become a reality.

Acknowledgements

This work has been (partially) funded by "CommSensLab" Excellence Research Unit Maria de Maeztu (MINECO grant MDM-2016-0600), the Spanish Ministerio MICINN and EU ERDF project "SPOT: Sensing with pioneering opportunistic techniques" (grant RTI2018-099008-B-C21/AEI/10.13039/501100011033), by the grant PID2019-106808-RA-I00/AEI/FEDER/UE from the EDRF and the Spanish Governement, and by the Secretaria d'Universitats i Recerca del Departament d'Empresa i Coneixement de la Generalitat de Catalunya (2017 SGR 376, and 2017 SGR 219).

Conflict of interest

The authors declare no conflict of interest.

Author details

Joan A. Ruiz-de-Azua[1,2,3*†], Anna Calveras[1†] and Adriano Camps[2†]

1 Department of Network Engineering, Universitat Politécnica de Catalunya – UPC BarcelonaTech, Barcelona, Spain

2 Department of Signal Theory and Communications, Universitat Politècnica de Catalunya – UPC BarcelonaTech, Barcelona, Spain

3 Institut d'Estudis Espacials de Catalunya (IEEC) - Research Group in Space Science and Technologies (CTE-UPC), Barcelona, Spain

*Address all correspondence to: ja.ruiz-de-azua@jarao.org

† These authors contributed equally.

IntechOpen

© 2021 The Author(s). Licensee IntechOpen. This chapter is distributed under the terms of the Creative Commons Attribution License (http://creativecommons.org/licenses/by/3.0), which permits unrestricted use, distribution, and reproduction in any medium, provided the original work is properly cited.

References

[1] Richard M Bentley and Albert T Owens. Syncom satellite program. *Journal of Spacecraft and Rockets*, 1(4): 395–399, 1964.

[2] Vittoria Mignone, Maria Angeles Vazquez-Castro, and Thomas Stockhammer. The future of satellite tv: The wide range of applications of the dvb-s2 standard and perspectives. *Proceedings of the IEEE*, 99(11): 1905–1921, 2011.

[3] Oriol Vidal, Greet Verelst, Jérôme Lacan, Eric Alberty, José Radzik, and Michel Bousquet. Next generation high throughput satellite system. In *2012 IEEE First AESS European Conference on Satellite Telecommunications (ESTEL)*, pages 1–7. IEEE, 2012.

[4] Stephen R Pratt, Richard A Raines, Carl E Fossa, and Michael A Temple. An operational and performance overview of the iridium low earth orbit satellite system. *IEEE Communications Surveys*, 2 (2):2–10, 1999. doi: 10.1109/COMST.1999.5340513.

[5] Robert A Wiedeman and Andrew J Viterbi. The globalstar mobile satellite system for worldwide personal communications. In *Proceedings 3rd International Mobile Satellite Conference, IMSC'93*, Pasadena, CA, USA, 1993.

[6] Eylem Ekici, Ian F Akyildiz, and Michael D Bender. Datagram routing algorithm for leo satellite networks. In *INFOCOM 2000. Nineteenth Annual Joint Conference of the IEEE Computer and Communications Societies. Proceedings. IEEE*, volume 2, pages 500–508. IEEE, 2000. doi: 10.1109/INFCOM.2000.832223.

[7] Markus Werner. A dynamic routing concept for atm-based satellite personal communication networks. *IEEE Journal on Selected Areas in Communications*, 15 (8):1636–1648, 1997. doi: 10.1109/49.634801.

[8] Ian Akyildiz, Eylem Ekici, and Michael Bender. Mlsr: a novel routing algorithm for multilayered satellite ip networks. *IEEE/ACM Transactions on networking*, 10(3):411–424, 2002. doi: 10.1109/TNET.2002.1012371.

[9] Cerf Vinton, Scott Burleigh, Adrian Hooke, Leigh Torgerson, Robert Durst, Keith Scott, Kevin Fall, and Howard Weiss. Delay-tolerant networking architecture. RFC 4838, RFC Editor, 2007.

[10] Alessandro Golkar and Ignasi Lluch. The federated satellite systems paradigm: Concept and business case evaluation. *Acta Astronautica*, 111: 230–248, 2015. doi: 10.1016/j.actaastro.2015.02.009.

[11] Golkar Alessandro and Alejandro Salado. Definition of New Space -Expert Survey Results and Key Technology Trends. *IEEE Journal on Miniaturization for Air and Space Systems*, pages 1–1, 2020. doi: 10.1109/JMASS.2020.3045851.

[12] Peter B. Selding. Worldvu, a satellite startup aiming to provide global internet connectivity, continues to grow absent clear google relationship. https://spacenews.com/41755worldvu-a-satellite-startupaiming-to-provide-global-internet/, 2014. [Online 17th July 2020].

[13] Dominic Gates. Elon musk touts launch of 'spacex seattle'. https://www.seattletimes.com/business/elon-musk-touts-launch-oflsquospacex-seattlersquo/, 2015. [Online 17th July 2020].

[14] Henry Caleb. Q&a — telesat's erwin hudson opens up about leo mega-constellation plans. https://spacenews.com/qa-telesats-erwin-hudson-opens-up-about-leomega-constellation-plans/, 2017. [Online 17th July 2020].

[15] Mark Harris. Why satellite mega-constellations are a threat to the future of space. https://www.technologyrevie

w.com/2019/03/29/136268/why-sate llitemega-constellations-are-a-massive threat-to-safety-in-space/, 2019. [Online 17th July 2020].

[16] Henry Caleb. Megaconstellation ventures cautious about deployment milestones. https://spacenews.com/ megaconstellation-ventures-cautious-aboutdeployment-milestones/, 2019. [Online 17th July 2020].

[17] Joan Adri'a Ruiz-de-Azua, Anna Calveras, and Adriano Camps. Internet of satellites (iosat): Analysis of network models and routing protocol requirements. *IEEE Access*, pages 20390–20411, 2018. doi: 10.1109/ ACCESS.2018.2823983.

[18] Oltjon Kodheli, Eva Lagunas, Nicola Maturo, Shree Krishna Sharma, Bhavani Shankar, JF Montoya, JC Duncan, Danilo Spano, Symeon Chatzinotas, Steven Kisseleff, et al. Satellite communications in the new space era: A survey and future challenges. *arXiv preprint arXiv:2002.08811*, 2020.

[19] 3GPP. Study on new radio (nr) to support non-terrestrial networks. Technical Report 3GPP TR 38.811 V15.1.0, 3rd Generation Partnership Project, 2019.

[20] Leah M Gaffney, Neal D Hulkower, and Leslie Klein. Non-geo mobile satellite systems: a risk assessment. *Space communications*, 14:123–129, 1996.

[21] Tatsuki Kashitani. Development and application of an analysis methodology for satellite broadband network architectures. In *20th AIAA International Communication Satellite Systems Conference and Exhibit*, page 2019, 2002.

[22] Aruna Balasubramanian, Brian Levine, and Arun Venkataramani. Dtn routing as a resource allocation problem. In *Proceedings of the 2007 conference on Applications, technologies, architectures, and protocols for computer communications*, pages 373–384, 2007.

[23] Mark W Maier. Architecting principles for systems-of-systems. *Systems Engineering: The Journal of the International Council on Systems Engineering*, 1(4):267–284, 1998.

[24] Yong Lu, Fuchun Sun, and Youjian Zhao. Virtual topology for leo satellite networks based on earth-fixed footprint mode. *IEEE communications letters*, 17 (2):357–360, 2013. doi: 10.1109/ LCOMM.2013.011113.122635.

[25] Jordi Puig-Suari, Clark Turner, and William Ahlgren. Development of the standard cubesat deployer and a cubesat class picosatellite. In *2001 IEEE aerospace conference proceedings (cat. No. 01TH8542)*, volume 1, pages 1–347. IEEE, 2001.

[26] Inigo del Portillo, Bruce G Cameron, and Edward F Crawley. A technical comparison of three low earth orbit satellite constellation systems to provide global broadband. *Acta Astronautica*, 159:123–135, 2019.

[27] Foust Jeff. Spacex surpasses 1,000-satellite mark in latest starlink launch. https://spacenews.com/spacex-adds-laser-crosslinks-to-polarstarlink-satellites/, 2021. [Online 30th January 2021].

[28] Jonathan O'Callaghan. The risky rush for mega constellations. https:// www.scientificamerican.com/article/ the-risky-rush-for-megaconstellations/, 2019. [Online 17th July 2020].

[29] Henry Caleb. Bankruptcy court frees payment to oneweb satellites to restart satellite manufacturing. https:// spacenews.com/bankruptcycourt-frees-payment-to-onewebsatellites-to-restart-satellitemanufacturing/, 2020. [Online 17th July 2020].

[30] Henry Caleb. After bankruptcy, oneweb's supply chain looking for new

ways to keep busy. https://spacenews.com/afterbankruptcy-onewebs-supply-chainlooking-for-new-ways-to-keep-busy/, 2020. [Online 17th July 2020].

[31] Jeff Foust. Megaconstellation ventures cautious about deployment milestones. https://spacenews.com/starlink-vsthe-astronomers/, 2020. [Online 17th July 2020].

[32] Foust Jeff. Starlink vs. the astronomers. https://spacenews.com/starlink-vsthe-astronomers/, 2020. [Online 30th January 2021].

[33] Eylem Ekici, Ian Akyildiz, and Michael D. Bender. A multicast routing algorithm for leo satellite ip networks. *IEEE/ACM Transactions On Networking*, 10(2):183–192, 2002. doi: 10.1109/90.993300.

[34] Joan Adria Ruiz-de-Azua, Victoria Ramirez, Hyuk Park, Anna Calveras, and Adriano Camps. Assessment of satellite contacts using predictive algorithms for autonomous satellite networks. *IEEE Access*, 2020.

[35] Joan Adria Ruiz-de-Azua, Anna Calveras, and Adriano Camps. A Novel Dissemination Protocol to Deploy Opportunistic Services in Federated Satellite Systems. *IEEE Access*, 8:142348–142365, 2020. doi: 10.1109/ACCESS.2020.3013655.

[36] Joan A. Ruiz-de Azua, Nicola Garzaniti, Alessandro Golkar, Anna Calveras, and Adriano Camps. Towards federated satellite systems and internet of satellites: The federation deployment control protocol. *Remote Sensing*, 2021. [In press].

[37] 3GPP. Release 15 description. Technical Report 3GPP TR 21.915 V15.0.0, 3rd Generation Partnership Project, 2019.

[38] ITU Radiocommunication Sector. Guidelines for evaluation of radio interface technologies for imt-2020. Technical Report ITU-R M.2412, International Telecommunication Union (ITU), 2017.

[39] Luigi Atzori, Antonio Iera, and Giacomo Morabito. The internet of things: A survey. *Computer networks*, 54 (15):2787–2805, 2010. doi: 10.1016/j.comnet.2010.05.010.

[40] ITU Radiocommunication Sector. Minimum requirements related to technical performance for imt-2020 radio interface(s). Technical Report ITU-R M.2410, International Telecommunication Union (ITU), 2017.

[41] Konstantinos Liolis, Alexander Geurtz, Ray Sperber, Detlef Schulz, Simon Watts, Georgia Poziopoulou, Barry Evans, Ning Wang, Oriol Vidal, Boris Tiomela Jou, et al. Use cases and scenarios of 5g integrated satellite-terrestrial networks for enhanced mobile broadband: The sat5g approach. *International Journal of Satellite Communications and Networking*, 37(2): 91–112, 2019.

[42] Henry Caleb. Lacuna space aims to ride iot wave with a 32-cubesat constellation. https://spacenews.com/lacuna-spaceaims-to-ride-iot-wave-with-a-32-cubesat-constellation/, 2019. [Online 31*th* January 2021].

Chapter 3

Management of Software-Defined Networking Powered by Artificial Intelligence

Jehad Ali and Byeong-hee Roh

Abstract

Separating data and control planes by Software-Defined Networking (SDN) not only handles networks centrally and smartly. However, through implementing innovative protocols by centralized controllers, it also contributes flexibility to computer networks. The Internet-of-Things (IoT) and the implementation of 5G have increased the number of heterogeneous connected devices, creating a huge amount of data. Hence, the incorporation of Artificial Intelligence (AI) and Machine Learning is significant. Thanks to SDN controllers, which are programmable and versatile enough to incorporate machine learning algorithms to handle the underlying networks while keeping the network abstracted from controller applications. In this chapter, a software-defined networking management system powered by AI (SDNMS-PAI) is proposed for end-to-end (E2E) heterogeneous networks. By applying artificial intelligence to the controller, we will demonstrate this regarding E2E resource management. SDNMS-PAI provides an architecture with a global view of the underlying network and manages the E2E heterogeneous networks with AI learning.

Keywords: Software-defined networking, Machine learning, 5G, Networks management, Artificial intelligence

1. Introduction

Due to the rapid development of Internet technology, network terminals have been widely spread. However, traditional network architectures have failed to adapt to future advances in communication and Internet technologies, resulting in heterogeneous networks. As a result, the existing network infrastructure was unable to keep up with the rapid changes of the Internet. A key feature of traditional network architectures is that the data and control planes are tightly coupled, which has some limitations. For example, if you want to change the network configuration, you need to configure each device independently across the entire network which is a daunting task.

Similarly, vendors are reluctant to provide the internal details of the device to developers and users, as changes in the configuration of existing networking devices can lead to malfunctions in the network. In addition, the protocol is strongly built into the firmware of network devices. These limitations hinder network innovation due to proprietary hardware and lack of testing for innovative networking solutions due to their distributed nature. It also increases the management workload and the overall cost of network management.

On the other hand, Software Defined Networking (SDN) [1–5] has revolutionized network management by separating data and control planes. The data plane is composed of forwarding devices, for example routers, switches, etc. Its main functions are forwarding the packets according to the policies of the controller. If the destination of the arrived packets is not found in the forwarding devices, then those packets are sent to the controller by the data plane. The control plane, however, is implemented through intelligent SDN controllers such as OpenDaylight (ODL), Open Networking Operating System (ONOS), POX and RYU [6]. Control plane obtains the status of the underlying network and defines the policies for the packets arriving on the forwarding devices. It then pushes the updated rules to the data plane. The separation of data and control planes has shifted network complexity from networking devices to smart SDN controllers. Thus, the network can be programmed through the application running on the controller and the underlying network is abstracted from the applications [7]. The innovative concept presented by SDN has the great advantage of flexible and efficient network configuration, network management and operation. Therefore, SDN is expected to be an excellent choice for the next generation of telecommunication networks and Internet technologies. Because of these benefits, large information technology organizations such as Facebook, Amazon, and Google have implemented SDN to connect remote data centers [8, 9].

The internet has grown in recent years. As a result, there is a huge increase in the amount of network traffic. Because the accuracy of machine learning algorithms depends mainly on the availability of historical data. There is therefore an increasing tendency towards the use of machine learning techniques. Because the accuracy of machine learning algorithms increases with sufficient data. For this reason, researchers now prefer to apply machine learning solutions because, once trained on the available data, the trained model generates accurate results on the new data through learning experience. The introduction of 5G heterogeneous networks and the rapid ubiquitous use and growth of Internet data processing requirements are rapidly increasing as a result of a dramatic increase in the number of connected devices. For example, the heterogeneous IoT devices in 5G runs different protocols and various technologies results in increasing the traffic load [10]. In addition, there is a need for self-organization and demand-based networks to deal with huge amounts of data. SDN was therefore at the heart of the growing needs of such applications due to their programming, orchestration, and automation characteristics [11].

The SDN has been successfully deployed in data centers and enterprise traffic engineering networks across remote data centers. However, the adoption of SDN in the modern and global Internet still presents a number of challenges that need further investigation. As the internet is scaling and the traffic on the underlying network is dynamically changing. The application of an optimum policy for the underlying network should therefore be adapted in line with the radical changes in the internet. One of the problems in SDN is the configuration of the control plane, because the manual configuration is a costly task, because the traditional SDN approach [12–15] is not optimal in selecting the optimum policy for the underlying network. In addition, repeatedly reconfiguring the policy according to changes in the network will require the control plane to be reconfigured. One of the main issues, therefore, is the automatic orchestration of the control plane [16]. Because the rigid configuration of the control plane will have problems in the optimal configuration of the policy.

Another issue is the end-to-end (E2E) quality-of-service (QoS) performance of heterogeneous network providers. If the same provider manages SDN controllers, user applications and forwarding devices on the enterprise network, then, the network status of the underlying devices is readily available for upper-layer applications. However, the Internet consists of different providers where end-users, applications and service providers are often heterogeneous. As a result, the status of the network is not directly available for applications running on the upper layers.

Several solutions have been proposed to address the issue of the allocation of E2E resources [17–23]. However, they depend on the traditional and manual configuration of the control plane. i.e., once a policy has been defined for the underlying network. The behavior of the network is then controlled accordingly, regardless of the scale of the network or the dynamic changes. The policy of controlling the network is therefore not always optimal. Moreover, these solutions do not provide effective management of the SDN due to scaling up, increasing network complexity and dynamic changes. There is therefore a need to find a global optimal solution with an excellent value for the objective functions. We therefore propose a software-defined networking management system powered by AI (SDNMS-PAI) architecture to auto-configure policy management and E2E resource allocation.

The advantage of AI based architecture is that the AI agent will interact with the underlying network through the SDN controller for pushing the global optimal policy flow rules in the forwarding devices. The controller will share the network status information with the AI agent and based on real time status of the network the AI agent will find the most appropriate actions to be taken. The actions will be pushed as the flow rules in the forwarding devices. AI can be used to bring a closed-loop control of the SDN. The closed-loop control incorporates collection of data, analytics, and subsequent actions that are all based on the results of the analytics [24]. All components of the closed loop can be improved and enhanced by means of AI to improve the speed, accuracy and, ultimately, the effectiveness of the closed loop control.

The main contributions of this chapter are summarized as follows:

- We leverage the hierarchical SDN architecture to provision the E2E QoS for heterogeneous networks and build a centralized intelligent agent with global E2E view aiming at learning the global optimum policy through interaction with the data plane.

- We apply Q-learning where the learning agent obtains the states of the underlying network and provisions the E2E resource allocations for a service request in the heterogeneous network domains with several QoS classes on the E2E path.

- We demonstrate the proposed SDNMS-PAI with a use case for E2E resource allocation i.e. E2E QoS provisioning.

- Moreover, we evaluate the E2E delay, jitter, packet loss ratio (PLR), and E2E degree of correspondence (DC) [25] ratio for service requests in a hierarchical SDN architecture with an AI agent.

2. AI powered SDN architecture

In this section, an overview of the proposed SDNMS-PAI is provided. First, we introduce the three planes of the SDN architecture and explain them with a pictorial diagram. Then, we introduce the hierarchical SDN architecture for the allocation of E2E resources and the deployment of AI enabled learning. The hierarchical control plane consists of two levels of hierarchy of local and global controllers. Then we develop the SDNMS-PAI architecture for the E2E view and the resource allocation leveraging Q-learning. The proposed architecture consists of a hierarchical control plane with a global E2E view and leverages Q-learning to manage E2E resources in SDN in a smart way.

2.1 Hierarchical control plane SDN architecture powered by AI

In this subsection, we first introduce an SDN and a hierarchical architecture followed by an AI powered SDN architecture. The SDN consists of data, control, and application planes. **Figure 1** [26] shows the typical SDN architecture. Forwarding devices like routers and switches are part of the data plane. The centralized controller is part of the control plane. At the top is the application plane where different applications can be deployed and executed for a variety of purposes, such as routing, load balancing, security, and monitoring. The controller shall act as a strategic control point for the underlying network. However, several issues arise from a single controller in the SDN. For example, if the controller fails due to a software or hardware problem, the entire network that depends on the controller will collapse.

In addition, the controller will experience a performance bottleneck if the number of switches in its domain increases or the request messages towards it increases. Furthermore, traffic loads are not evenly distributed over the network. As a result,

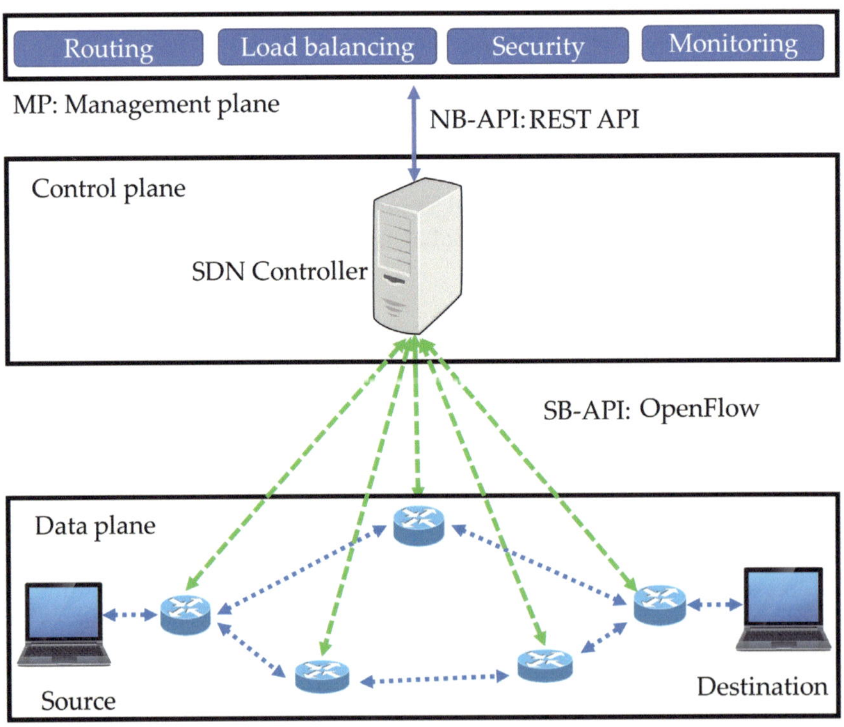

Figure 1.
SDN architecture [26].

multiple controllers should be used for viewing the E2E network. However, if there are multiple heterogeneous domains, there is a need for consistency and collaboration between domains for the provisioning of E2E QoS.

Figure 2 shows the hierarchical control plane SDN architecture. In the proposed architecture there are local controllers which has access of the data planes of the local domains. Global controllers (GCs) in the hierarchical control plane architecture have access to the global view of physically distributed local data plane switches. The hierarchical architecture of SDN controllers integrates autonomous domains with hierarchical associations. Multiple domains are integrated with the hierarchical architecture of the controller, where the local domain controllers (LCs) coordinate via the GC. By applying hierarchical architecture, new services can be easily managed and deployed in domains that coexist on the E2E path between the source and the destination [27] nodes.

The tasks handled by the controller are propagated from the lower LC layer to the upper GC layer, which reduces computational complexity. The hierarchical control plane with a global view reduces the E2E delay as the network scales [28]. In the proposed architecture, the GC acts proactively to set up the E2E path and therefore reduces the delay in setting up the path (the delay in setting up the path and pushing the flow entries into the switches) [29]. The hierarchical architecture enables communication between multiple LCs with a variety of equipment. The effectiveness of the hierarchical control plane for effective collaboration between heterogeneous tactical networks with a guaranteed QoS has been demonstrated in [30, 31]. The rewards for state action pairs in the Q-learning are therefore more accurate than the local view states because these rewards with a hierarchical architecture reflect the E2E view of the underlying network.

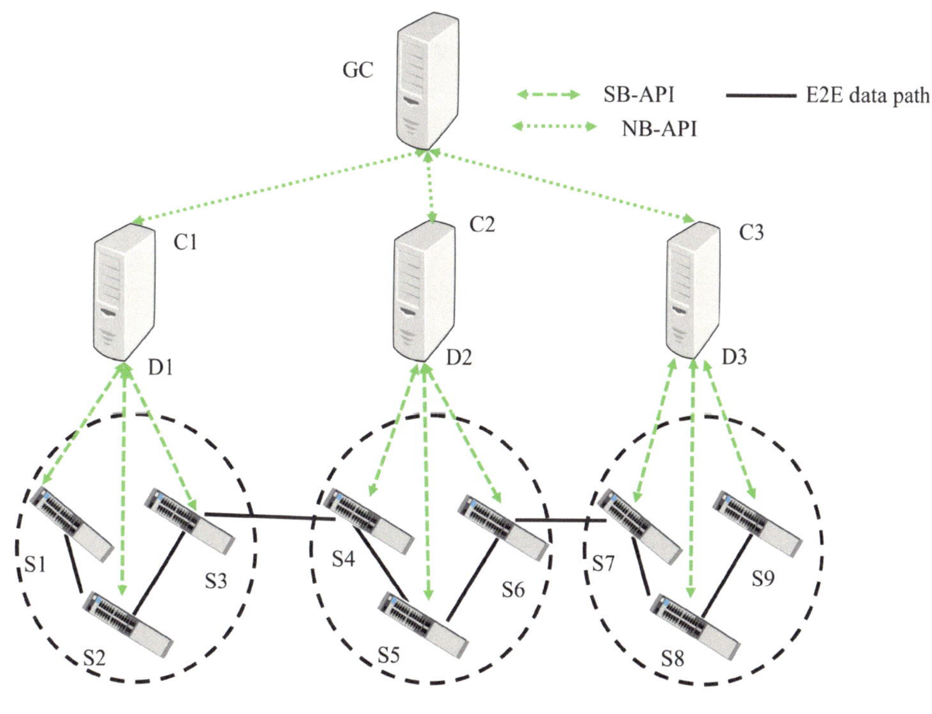

Figure 2.
SDN architecture with a global view of the E2E network [32, 33].

In our proposed SDNMS-PAI, a hierarchical control plane architecture is employed to construct a completely global view and control for geographical distributed network and build a global AI agent through the global control plane to generate a network control policy via reinforcement learning algorithms. The SDNMS-PAI can intelligently control and optimize a network to meet the differentiated network requirements in a large-scale dynamic network. In the following subsections, we describe the proposed AI enabled SDN architecture from bottom to top. The SDNMS-PAI is shown in **Figure 3**.

2.1.1 Data plane

Data plane in the SDNMS-PAI consists of the forwarding devices (known as the infrastructure or the underlying network). The matching of the packets in the data plane and the actions take place according to the forwarding rules that are defined in a flow Table. A flow table comprises of several flow entries. The packet header information is matched with the flow entries in the flow table. Each flow entry has three mandatory fields, i.e., header, action, and counter. **Table 1** is an example of a flow table in which the first row contains header fields and second and onward rows contain flow entries.

When a new packet arrives on the ingress port of a switch, the matching process starts, if a packet has a destination IP address starting with 172.10.X.X then forward it to port number 8 and counter 201 will be updated. Similarly, the third row (with source IP address: 10.10.1.X) explains if a packet has the same source and destination port number (X) then drop it. If the rules for the new packet do not exist in the flow table then the switch sends a Packet_In message to the controller and the destination will be returned by the controller to the forwarding device (Packet_Out message) and the flow rules will be updated in the flow table, respectively. In contrast to traditional networks where the decision about the routing takes place in the tightly couple distributed networking devices. Herein, in the SDNMS-PAI, the information of the network is collected via the LCs which is used by the AI enabled

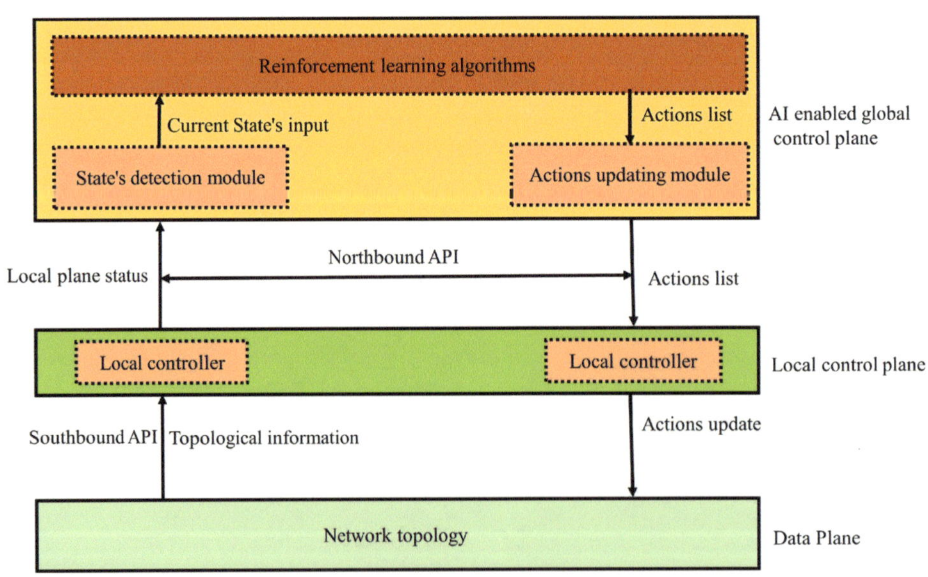

Figure 3.
AI powered SDN architecture for E2E resource allocation.

Source (IP address)	Destination (IP address)	Source (Port)	Destination (Port)	Action	Counter
X	172.10.X.X	X	X	Port 8	201
X	X	10	40	Drop	80
10.10.1.X	X	X	X	Drop	90
X	X	30	70	Port 3	100

Table 1.
An example of the flow table entries.

global control plane (AIGCP) for deciding about the global optimum policy and E2E resources allocation.

2.1.2 SB-API

The Southbound Application Programming Interface (SB-API) provides an interface for data interaction with the local control plane. There are several protocols available for the interaction of the two planes, but the most popular is OpenFlow. OpenFlow provides a secure interface for communication between the controller and the switch. The status of the network topology and the policies for action from the global control plane are communicated to the data plane via the SB-API in the SDNMS-PAI. The White Paper [34] describes the advantages and flexibility of OpenFlow for the programming of forwarding devices. The concept of OpenFlow originated from Stanford University, and the OpenFlow Networking Foundation (ONF) consortium now performs the standardization tasks of OpenFlow.

2.1.3 Local control plane

The data plane switches of each domain are connected to the LCs on the E2E path. The LCs interact with the data plane through SB-APIs. The AIGCP dynamically obtains the underlying network status from the LCs; therefore, it has access to the global topology. As a result, the AIGCP will provide resources from local controllers upon the arrival of a service request. LCs work together through GC, and service level agreements (SLAs) are exchanged through it. Each LC is equipped with a traffic flow template (TFT) module [35] containing the source and destination port numbers, the Internet Protocol (IP) addresses and the QoS parameters. The data collected will be used by the AIGCP for the allocation of E2E resources.

2.1.4 NB-API

The northbound application programming interface (NB-API) functions as a communication interface between the local control and AIGCP. The local control plane functions as a bridge between the forwarding devices and AIGCP utilizing the representational state transfer (REST) API. Similarly, the operational statistics (e.g., about the flow entries) from the data plane are available via this API to the global control plane AI agent. Reinforcement learning algorithms running in the global control plane communicates with the local control plane through this API and the corresponding actions are delegated to the data plane. These actions represent the behavior of the reinforcement learning algorithms executed in the global control plane. For example, a firewall application implements policies for controlling the ingress and egress packets passing through the network. Therefore, the data plane devices will forward or block the traffic according to the rules defined in the application. Similarly, a load balancing algorithm will control the traffic through monitoring congestion in different paths of the network. Herein, we employ the Q-learning for E2E QoS provisioning.

2.1.5 AI enabled global control plane

The purpose of the AIGCP is to generate global optimum policies leveraging the global view from the hierarchical SDN architecture. In the SDNMS-PAI paradigm, the AIGCP leverage of hierarchical SDN architecture to obtain the global view as well as control of the E2E network. The state detection module in the global control plane has the global view of the E2E network status which helps the AI agent to make decisions about the global optimum policy based on the E2E view. It feeds the AI agent with the information about the states of the E2E network.

2.1.6 Optimal policy learning mechanism

The local controllers obtain the QoS information (such as the delay, jitter, and PLR) from the data plane devices for all the service requests and the service classes on the E2E paths. The service requests and service classes are shown in **Table 2** [36] and **Table 3** [37]. The service request is a combination of the E2E delay, jitter, and PLR for an application. An example of the offered service classes in 5 E2E domains is shown in **Table 3**. Each local controller shares this information with the global controller. Thus, global controller has the E2E view of the network.

Reinforcement learning with Q-learning enabled AI agent is used to maximize the rewards for an agent. Q-learning is one of the methodologies to leverage reinforcement learning. It does not require a model of the environment, and it can cope with problems utilizing stochastic transitions with rewards, without demanding adaptations. For a finite Markov decision process (FMDP), Q-learning computes an optimal policy aiming to maximize the expected value of the accumulated reward over every as well as all successive steps, beginning from current state. Q-learning can find an optimal action-selection policy for any given FMDP, given infinite exploration time along with partly-random policy [38]. Q is the function name that the algorithm learns with the maximum expected rewards for an action taken in a given state [39].

If the service request meets the end-to-end QoS demand for a state action pair, a high reward factor is assigned. For this purpose, the *DC* ratio is checked for the state action pair. The *DC* ratio denotes whether the QoS requirements are meeting for a service request or not. For example, if the application service request E2E demand for delay is 150 and the service classes offer a delay of 40, 20, 15, 0 and 45 on the E2E path, then the ratio will be 150/120 i.e., 1.25. Hence, if the $DC>1$ it is awarded

Metric	Service Requests for an application		
	1	2	3
Delay (ms)	150	200	400
Jitter (ms)	60	60	80
PLR	10^{-4}	10^{-3}	10^{-3}

Table 2.
An example of the E2E service requests.

Domain	QoS Class	Offered Delay (ms)	Offered jitter (ms)	Offered PLR
1	1	40	10	10^{-5}
	2	80	30	10^{-4}
	3	120	0	10^{-4}
2	1	20	15	10^{-6}
	2	50	20	10^{-5}
	3	70	30	5×10^{-5}
	4	120	0	10^{-4}
3	1	15	10	10^{-6}
	2	50	30	10^{-5}
4	1	12	6	10^{-5}
	2	0	0	10^{-4}
5	1	45	5	10^{-5}
	2	100	15	10^{-4}
	3	120	40	10^{-4}

Table 3.
An example of the service classes on the E2E path passing through five domains.

a high Q value for the service request. On the contrary if the $DC<1$, the reward is low for the state action pair for that service request. This process continues until all the possible source to destination paths are explored and checked for the DC value against each state action pair.

3. Use case

Herein, we describe a scenario in which we can employ our proposed SDNMS-PAI for modeling the behavior of the network. We provide an example in the context of QoS service classes allocation, where the SDNMS-PAI is used to make smart choices in order to choose the best service classes on the E2E routing path to meet the E2E QoS requirements. Moreover, based on the Q-learning rewards more excellent service classes are selected in future. The traditional design of the internet mainly focusses on the reliability of services [16]. However, with 5G and beyond networks the requirements for applications have changed, and the applications demands for low latency with high data rates. Further, it is imperative whether the E2E QoS is according to the application service requests. Moreover, with heterogeneous networks on the path from source to destination, there exists several service classes in each domain. Hence, meeting the E2E QoS requirements for the applications service requests is a challenging problem.

Service class mapping mainly involves service classes allocation on the E2E path that meets the QoS demands of different service requests. The typical E2E service classes request for each application are different as shown in **Table 2**. For example, for application 1 the service requests are different than from application 2 and so on. Several solutions [40–42] have been proposed by researchers for service class mapping to meet the E2E QoS requirements for the applications. Furthermore, the mapping of the service classes is a challenging task with respect to meeting the E2E service needs due to the local view of the network state information in the domains.

4. Results and discussion

Results of the proposed SDNMS-PAI are compared with existing ones i.e., software-defined networking with no artificial intelligence (SDN-NAI) [32]. There are 5 domains on the E2E path and two layers of the controllers i.e., local controllers and a global controller. We consider delay, jitter, and PLR as the primary QoS parameters in every domain. Controllers of the five domains are assigned to 50 nodes according to the controller placement in [43].

Figure 4 compares the E2E delay (in milliseconds (ms)) from source to destination for the SDN-NAI i.e., SDN with no artificial intelligence enabled global control plane and our proposed SDNMS-PAI with. We can see that the delay for the initial service requests is greater for the SDNMS-PAI because the AI agent explores the E2E paths from source to destination for the optimal service classes. However, as the AI agent learns about the global optimum policy, then the delay decrease as compared to SDN-NAI which is shown in the 3rd, 4th' and 5th domains. Initially the service request rates are smaller hence the delay is low however with increasing the service request rate the delay increases because of the consumption of the available bandwidth resources on the E2E paths.

The results in **Figure 5** show that E2E jitter (ms) from source to destination for an SDN-NAI compared with SDNMS-PAI. The figure reveals that the jitter for the initial service requests is greater for the SDNMS-PAI due to the AI agent exploring the E2E paths from source to destination to find the optimal service classes. However, as the AI agent becomes more proficient in learning about the global optimum policy, then the jitter decreases as compared to SDN-NAI, which is shown in the 3rd, 4th, and 5th domains. Initially, with lower service request rate the jitter is low since each service request requires only a portion of the available bandwidth on an E2E path. With increasing the service request rate, however, the jitter will increase because of the bandwidth resources used in each service request.

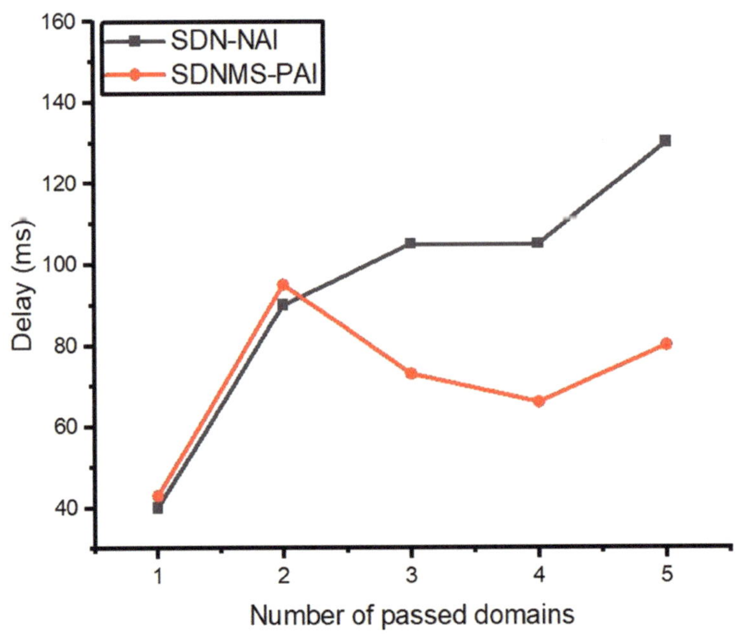

Figure 4.
E2E delay from source to destination with increasing service requests passing through five domains.

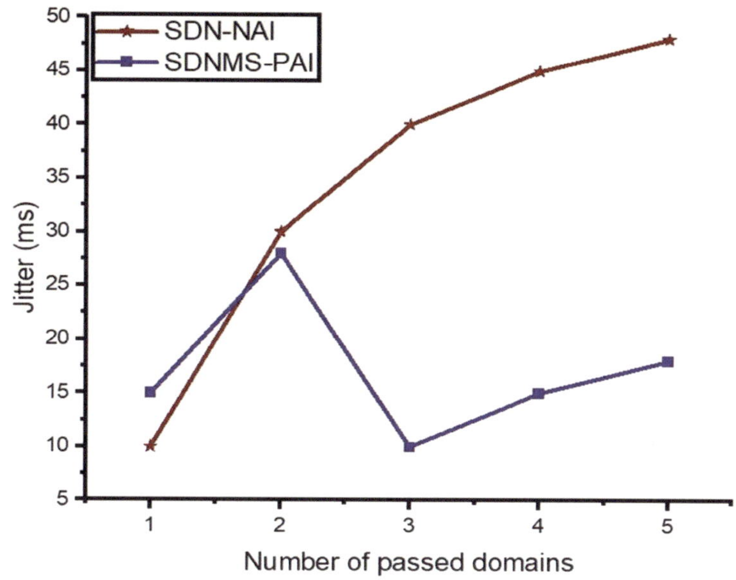

Figure 5.
E2E jitter from source to destination with increasing service requests passing through five domains.

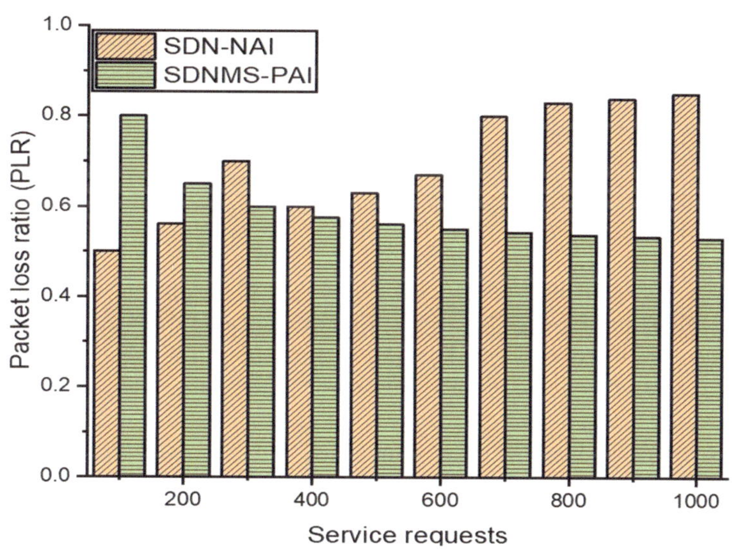

Figurc 6.
Packet loss ratio (PLR) with increasing service request rate.

Figure 6 compares the PLR with increasing the service request rate. Herein, the PLR is the ratio of the number of received packets divided by the total number of packets against each service request from source to destination. We can see from **Figure 6** that the PLR is initially high for the SDNMS-PAI however as the AI agent obtains a global optimum then the PLR does not increase in the same rate with SDN-NAI. However, the overall PLR increase with increasing the service request rate because the available resources in the network gets occupied.

Figure 7 shows a comparison of the E2E DC ratio for SDNMS-PAI and SDN-NAI. We can see from the figure that the SDN-NAI DC ratio was initially higher than the SDNMS-PAI. However, as the AI agent learns, the DC ratio for the proposed scheme is much higher than the SDN-NAI ratio. The basic reason is that, as the service

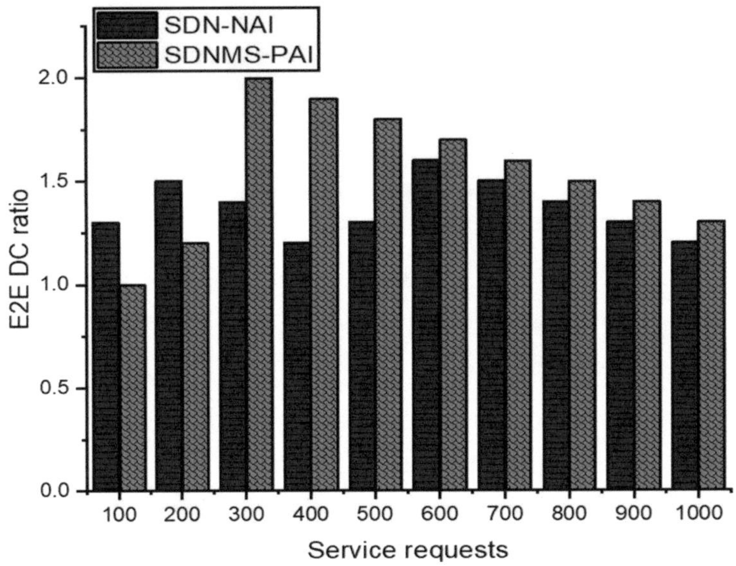

Figure 7.
E2E DC ratio against service requests.

requests increase, the overall DC ratio becomes low due to the consumption of the available bandwidth on the E2E pathways. Nevertheless, the E2E DC ratio is still 1 or greater than 1 for the proposed SDNMS-PAI, which means that it satisfies the QoS requirements for the application service request. In addition, it overcomes the SDN-NAI in E2E DC ratio.

5. Conclusions

In this chapter we proposed SDNMS-PAI for the E2E resource allocation i.e., service classes allocation for the E2E service requests. As the distributed management and tight coupling of control and data planes limit the control and global view of network resources. Moreover, the E2E resources in heterogeneous networks cannot be provisioned. Hence, in this chapter we proposed the hierarchical SDN architecture because a single controller with manual configuration of the control plane led to failure and restricts the optimal policy. Moreover, we provided a use case example with service requests and service classes. Furthermore, the SDNMS-PAI scheme employed in a hierarchical SDN architecture with AI agent in the global control plane overcomes the SDN-NAI in terms of E2E delay, jitter, PLR, and DC ratio.

Acknowledgements

This was supported by the Ministry of Science and ICT (MSIT), South Korea, through the Information Technology Research Center (ITRC) Support Program, supervised by the Institute for Information and Communications Technology Planning and Evaluation, under Grant IITP-2021-2018-0-01431.

Conflict of interest

The authors declare no conflict of interest.

DOI: http://dx.doi.org/10.5772/intechopen.97197

Author details

Jehad Ali and Byeong-hee Roh*
Department of Computer Engineering, and Department of AI Convergence Network, Ajou University, Suwon, South Korea

*Address all correspondence to: bhroh@ajou.ac.kr

IntechOpen

© 2021 The Author(s). Licensee IntechOpen. This chapter is distributed under the terms of the Creative Commons Attribution License (http://creativecommons.org/licenses/by/3.0), which permits unrestricted use, distribution, and reproduction in any medium, provided the original work is properly cited. (cc) BY

References

[1] Ahmad S, Mir AH. Scalability, Consistency, Reliability and Security in SDN Controllers: A Survey of Diverse SDN Controllers. Journal of Network and Systems Management. 2021 Jan;29(1):1-59. DOI: 10.1007/s10922-020-09575-4

[2] Sarmiento D, Lebre A, Nussbaum L, Chari A. Decentralized SDN Control Plane for a Distributed Cloud-Edge Infrastructure: A Survey. IEEE Communications Surveys & Tutorials. 2021;:1-1. DOI: 10.1109/COMST.2021.3050297.

[3] Singh S, Jha RK. A survey on software defined networking: Architecture for next generation network. Journal of Network and Systems Management. 2017 Apr 1;25(2):321-74.

[4] Tadros CN, Rizk MR, Mokhtar BM. Software defined network-based management for enhanced 5G network services. IEEE Access. 2020 Mar 12;8:53997-4008.

[5] Long Q, Chen Y, Zhang H, Lei X. Software Defined 5G and 6G Networks: a Survey. Mobile Networks and Applications. 2019;.

[6] Ali J, Lee S, Roh BH. Performance analysis of POX and Ryu with different SDN topologies. InProceedings of the 2018 International Conference on Information Science and System 2018 Apr 27 (pp. 244-249).

[7] McKeown N, Anderson T, Balakrishnan H, Parulkar G, Peterson L, Rexford J, Shenker S, Turner J. OpenFlow: enabling innovation in campus networks. ACM SIGCOMM computer communication review. 2008 Mar 31;38(2):69-74.

[8] Jain S, Kumar A, Mandal S, Ong J, Poutievski L, Singh A, Venkata S, Wanderer J, Zhou J, Zhu M, Zolla J. B4: Experience with a globally-deployed software defined WAN. ACM SIGCOMM Computer Communication Review. 2013 Aug 27;43(4):3-14.

[9] Ali J, Roh BH, Lee S. QoS improvement with an optimum controller selection for software-defined networks. Plos one. 2019 May 31;14(5):e0217631.

[10] Kazmi SA, Khan LU, Tran NH, Hong CS. Network slicing for 5G and beyond networks. Springer International Publishing; 2019 May 14.

[11] Ali J, Roh BH, Lee B, Oh J, Adil M. A Machine Learning Framework for Prevention of Software-Defined Networking controller from DDoS Attacks and dimensionality reduction of big data. International Conference on Information and Communication Technology Convergence (ICTC), Jeju Island, Korea (South), 2020, 515-519, DOI: 10.1109/ICTC49870.2020.9289504.

[12] Duan Q. End-to-end service delivery with QoS guarantee in software defined networks. Transactions on Networks and Communications. 2018; 6(2), p. 10, 2018.

[13] Mendiola A, Astorga J, Jacob E, Stamos K. Enhancing network resources utilization and resiliency in multi-domain bandwidth on demand service provisioning using SDN. Telecommunication Systems. 2019 Jul;71(3):505-15.

[14] Francesco L, Marchetto G, Risso F, Santuari M, Gerola M. A Proposal for End-to-End QoS Provisioning in Software-Defined Networks. International Journal of Electrical and Computer Engineering (IJECE). 2017; 7(4), 2261-2277. DOI: 10.11591/ijece.v7i4.pp2261-2277

[15] Egilmez HE, Dane ST, Bagci KT, Tekalp AM. OpenQoS: An OpenFlow controller design for multimedia delivery with end-to-end Quality of Service over Software-Defined Networks. InProceedings of the 2012 Asia Pacific signal and information processing association annual summit and conference 2012 Dec 3 (pp. 1-8). IEEE.

[16] Yao H, Jiang C, Qian Y. Developing Networks Using Artificial Intelligence. Springer International Publishing; 2019 Apr 26.

[17] Alshaer H, Haas H. Software-Defined Networking-Enabled Heterogeneous Wireless Networks and Applications Convergence. IEEE Access. 2020 Apr 6;8:66672-92.

[18] Ibarra-Lancheros KS, Puerto-Leguizamón G, Suárez-Fajardo C. Quality of service evaluation based on network slicing for software-defined 5G systems. TecnoLogicas. 2018 Dec;21(43):27-41.

[19] Bagci KT, Tekalp AM. SDN-enabled distributed open exchange: Dynamic QoS-path optimization in multi-operator services. Computer Networks. 2019 Oct 24;162:106845.

[20] Das D, Bapat J, Das D. A dynamic QoS negotiation mechanism between wired and wireless SDN domains. IEEE Transactions on Network and Service Management. 2017 Sep 25;14(4):1076-85.

[21] Joshi KD, Kataoka K. PRIME-Q: Privacy aware End-to-end QoS framework in multi-domain SDN. In2019 IEEE Conference on Network Softwarization (NetSoft) 2019 Jun 24 (pp. 169-177). IEEE.

[22] F. Lucrezia, G. Marchetto, F. Risso, M. Santuari, and M. Gerola, "A proposal for End-to-end QoS provisioning in software-defined networks," Int. J. Electr. Comput. Eng. (IJECE), vol. 7, no. 4, pp. 2261-2277, 2017.

[23] Karakus M, Durresi A. A scalable inter-as qos routing architecture in software defined network (sdn). In2015 IEEE 29th International Conference on Advanced Information Networking and Applications 2015 Mar 24 (pp. 148-154). IEEE.

[24] Gilbert M. Artificial Intelligence for Autonomous Networks; 2020 June 30.

[25] Stojanovic MD, Rakas SV, Acimovic-Raspopovic VS. End-to-end quality of service specification and mapping: The third party approach. Computer Communications. 2010 Jul 1;33(11):1354-68.

[26] Ali J, Lee GM, Roh BH, Ryu DK, Park G. Software-Defined Networking Approaches for Link Failure Recovery: A Survey. Sustainability. 2020 Jan;12(10):4255.

[27] Li LE, Mao ZM, Rexford J. Toward software-defined cellular networks. In2012 European workshop on software defined networking 2012 Oct 25 (pp. 7-12). IEEE.

[28] Elgendi I, Munasinghe KS, Jamalipour A. A three-tier SDN architecture for DenseNets. In2015 9th International Conference on Signal Processing and Communication Systems (ICSPCS) 2015 Dec 14 (pp. 1-7). IEEE.

[29] Khalili R, Despotovic Z, Hecker A. Flow setup latency in SDN networks. IEEE Journal on Selected Areas in Communications. 2018 Sep 19;36(12):2631-9.

[30] Elgendi I, Munasinghe KS, Mcgrath B. A heterogeneous software defined networking architecture for the tactical edge. In2016 Military Communications and Information Systems Conference (MilCIS) 2016 Nov 8 (pp. 1-7). IEEE.

[31] Ali J, Roh BH. Quality of Service Improvement with Optimal Software-Defined Networking Controller and Control Plane Clustering, cmc-computers materials & continua. 2021. 67(1), 849-875, DOI:10.32604/cmc.2021.014576

[32] Ali J, Roh BH. An Effective Hierarchical Control Plane for Software-Defined Networks Leveraging TOPSIS for End-to-End QoS Class-Mapping. IEEE Access. 2020 May 11;8:88990-9006.

[33] Ali J, Roh BH. A Framework for QoS-aware Class Mapping in Multi-domain SDN. In2019 IEEE 10th Annual Information Technology, Electronics and Mobile Communication Conference (IEMCON) 2019 Oct 17 (pp. 0602-0606). IEEE.

[34] Lara A, Kolasani A, Ramamurthy B. Network innovation using openflow: A survey. IEEE communications surveys & tutorials. 2013 Aug 30;16(1):493-512.

[35] Bilen T, Canberk B, Chowdhury KR. Handover management in software-defined ultra-dense 5G networks. IEEE Network. 2017 Jul 28;31(4):49-55.

[36] *Network Performance Objectives for IP-Based Services*, Standard ITU-T Recommendation Y.1541, 2011.

[37] Mali BJ, Ninkovic NM, Stojanovic MD, Savic GI. Service class mapping based on integer programming algorithm in the third party agent. In2014 22nd Telecommunications Forum Telfor (TELFOR) 2014 Nov 25 (pp. 170-173). IEEE.

[38] Melo, Francisco S. "Convergence of Q-learning: a simple proof"

[39] Matiisen, Tambet (December 19, 2015). "Demystifying Deep Reinforcement Learning". neuro.cs.ut.ee. Computational Neuroscience Lab. Accessed 2018-04-06.

[40] Stojanovic MD, Rakas SV. Policies for allocating performance impairment budgets among multiple IP providers. AEU-International Journal of Electronics and Communications. 2013 Mar 1;67(3):206-16.

[41] Mali BJ, Ninkovic NM, Stojanovic MD, Savic GI. Service class mapping based on integer programming algorithm in the third party agent. In2014 22nd Telecommunications Forum Telfor (TELFOR) 2014 Nov 25 (pp. 170-173). IEEE.

[42] Ninkovic NM, Mali BJ, Stojanovic MD, Savic GI. Multi-objective third-party approach for service class mapping among multiple providers in the internet. Elektronika ir Elektrotechnika. 2015 Apr 9;21(2):80-4.

[43] Wang G, Zhao Y, Huang J, Wu Y. An effective approach to controller placement in software defined wide area networks. IEEE Transactions on Network and Service Management. 2017 Dec 20;15(1):344-55.

Section 2

Healthcare Industry

Chapter 4

Smart Health and Cybersecurity in the Era of Artificial Intelligence

A.K.M. Jahangir Alam Majumder and Charles B. Veilleux

Abstract

The need for a transformation in providing healthcare has been recognized by organizations and captured in reports. Research into Smart Health using Artificial Intelligence (AI) could help identify the mental health of individuals by analyzing physiological data. The complexity of emotions can make it challenging for an individual to recognize they are coping with mental illness. AI could be used as an objective method in recognizing mental health crisis. This is where smart emotion could help as a Human-in-the-loop system that can reduce the time it takes for an individual to get treatment by identifying mental illness. Early treatment of mental health crises can lead to an overall reduction in damage caused by it. Further, COVID-19 has overwhelmed many healthcare systems, leading malicious actors to target them, highlighting many Cybersecurity issues. AI could aid in addressing Cybersecurity concerns to create a robust and secure Human-in-the-Loop system for mental health problems.

Keywords: COVID-19, Cybersecurity, Smart Health, Human-in-the-loop, IoT, CPS, AI

1. Introduction

Given the frequency and the intensity of healthcare-related incidents, Artificial intelligence (AI) applications and cybersecurity threats in healthcare are all the rage now [1]. Cybersecurity is the process of protecting computer systems, networks, and programs from any unauthorized access. Cyberattacks have become more sophisticated using AI to get past cyber defenses. The AI is also being used to constantly manage and secure the increasing number of healthcare Internet of Things (IoT) sensor nodes and Cyber Physical Systems (CPS) devices as they connect and disconnect from hospital networks [2]. The CPS is intelligent system consisting of cyber and physical components which is controlled and monitored by AI algorithm. With the development of smart multisensory systems, sensorial media, smart things, and cloud technologies, "Smart healthcare" is getting notable attention from academia, government, industry, caregivers, and healthcare communities [3–9]. In the recent smart health technological revolution, IoT technology playing an important role in healthcare for it's ability to predict, prevent, and intelligently control the the emerging infectious diseas like, Coronavirus (Covid-19). Also, IoT has introduced the vision of a smarter world into a reality with large datasets and services [10–13]. The AI-driven IoT has become more popular in smart healthcare system by utilizing machine learning algorithms and by providing a better understanding of healthcare information to support improved personalized healthcare during the epidemic of Covid-19 [14–16]. Also, it can support powerful processing and storage capacity of enormous datasets from IoT sensors and actuators as well as to provide automated decision making in real-time. A very little attention is given to developing a secure affordable healthcare system while the study of AI and cybersecurity for smart healthcare have been making great innovations in the age of Covid-19. The AI-driven IoT (AIIoT) for smart healthcare has the potential to revolutionize many aspects of our healthcare industry. AI-based analytics for secure smart health infrastructure is shown in **Figure 1**.

The importance of secure transformation in medical, public health, and healthcare delivery approaches have been recognized by numerous organizations [17]. The Networking and Information Technology Research and Development (NITRD) program recently has published the Federal Health Information Technology Research and Development Strategic Framework. This framework has explained the importance of the integration between the computing, engineering, mathematics and statistics, behavioral and social science, and public health research communities to explore the essential innovation to improve the services in the healthcare system [18]. Recent significant advances in machine learning (ML), artificial intelligence (AI), deep learning, high-performance cloud computing, and the availability of new datasets make such integration achievable.

Transformative approach can help to develop computational approaches for the analysis of multilevel and multiscale personal and clinical health data to maximize the accuracy of data implications. The transformative data science, mainly focuses on science and engineering innovations by interdisciplinary teams and utilize the advance sensing methods to intuitively and intelligently collect, connect, analyze and interpret data from individuals, device, and systems. Also, this integrated and intelligent data collection will help to optimize the healthcare services. The challenges include a number of issues from data collection, synchronization, fusion, and visualization of multisensory systems, electronic health records (EHRs), and medical and consumer devices. Underlying these challenges are many fundamentals issues, such as interoperability, integration, and reuse of heterogeneous data, feature selection, optimization, uncertainty quantification, robustness, model validation and evaluation, data privacy, and most importantly physical and cybersecurity. A robust research study might help to address how predictive, rigorous models with uncertainty can be build from sensory or EHR data for validation and testing and to improve the reproducibility of model building and simulations [18].

The World Health Organization (WHO) defines Smarthealthcare as "Information and Communication Technology applications in the healthcare, including disease

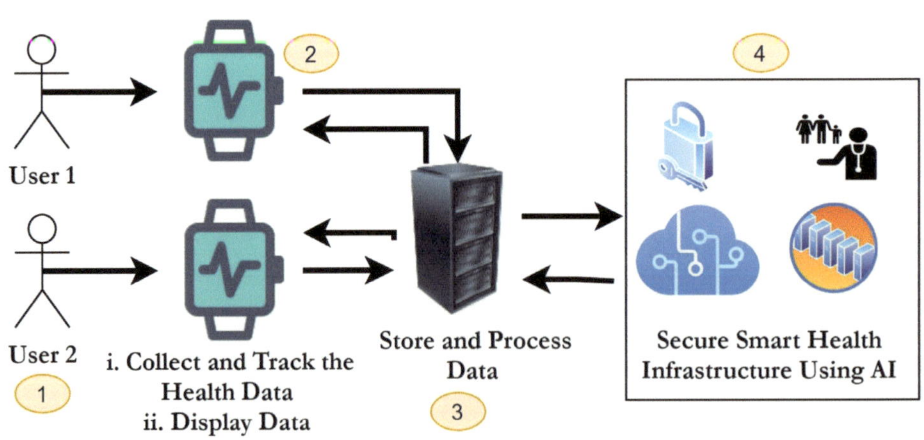

Figure 1.
AI-based Analytics for Secure Smart Health Infrastructure.

control and monitoring, education, and research". Additionally, scientists state that "Smart Healthcare" is the integration of health informatics, public health, and business applications through the internet and related AI and data mining techniques. The above mentioned techniques can provide more security and high accuracy in personalized healthcare and health informatics. Though the deep learning concept becomes popular, the scientists have rarely used this technique to predict outcomes from multisensory health data. They prefer to make the healthcare prediction using algorithm based on statistical methods and regression analysis [19–21]. In this chapter, the authors discussed the importance and challenges of using AI for cybersecurity vulnerabilities that have compromised the confidentiality, integrity, and availability of data for the affected healthcare systems in the age of Covid-19.

2. Cybersecurity for smart health

2.1 Healthcare Cybersecurity In The Age of COVID-19

Healthcare is one of the most vulnerable industries when it comes to cybersecurity. The healthcare system around the globe has become more susceptible to cyber attacks in the age of COVID-19. Many cyber-security organizations are reporting a rapid increase in cyber attacks since the start of the COVID-19 pandemic. The healthcare system, including nursing home, has always been one of the key target of cyberattacks. Recent string of attacks in several major hospitals and healthcare systems, have exposed the security vulnerabilities of most trusted healthcare institutions. The healthcare industries are at forefront of global efforts to fight the virus (COVID-19) during the pandemic. As such, this critical sector should be secure by cybercriminals, but that is not what has happened. The COVID-19 era is characterized by a steep rise in cyber attacks, from different perpetrators and for different motivations, and the healthcare sector has not been secure [22]. The smart health pipeline for data processing and security analytics using AI is shown in **Figure 2**.

Security and privacy in the healthcare industry are very crucial as they involve a patient's/user's personal information and private medical records. During the last few decades, the healthcare provider has increased the use of advanced technologies, like Artificial Intelligence (AI), machine learning techniques to secure patients' health profiles, storing data in the cloud, advanced medical devices, etc. These technological advancements have reduced the work of healthcare providers and have led to a paperless environment. But in return, the risk of cyber-attacks has increased. In most of the cases, there are no appropriate security systems installed to protect the hospital database, and the healthcare provider are often unaware of the cybersecurity threats lie in the shadows. Information Technology (IT) in

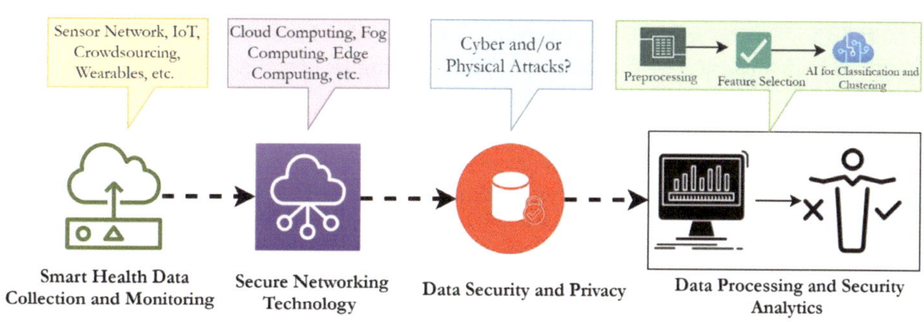

Figure 2.
Smart Health Pipeline.

healthcare systems is vulnerable to the point that it can take even several weeks before a cyberattack is acknowledged. The healthcare providers continue working with a hacked system without having any knowledge of the attacks. This could result in spending billions of dollars and affect millions of patients each year [23].

In the last few years, the healthcare industry has been exposed to several cyberattacks. The most significant cyberattacks among them are:

2.1.1 Cyberattack on UVM Health Network

The University of Vermont (UVM) Healthcare system was shut down after identifying a cyberattack on Oct. 28, 2020. The hospital was losing about $1.5 million per day, including lost revenue from postponed services and expenses needed to recover from the attack. The healthcare system was shut down for about 40 days including electronic health records (HER). More than 5000 computers were infected as they all were connected to the same network. In November, about three hundred employees were not able to work during this outage. UVM Medical Center President and COO Stephen Leffler, MD, said the health system expects the entire incident will cost more than $63 million by the time it resolves [24].

2.1.2 Ryuk and NHSD ransomware attack

On Oct. 26, 2020, an adversary attack (Ryuk ransomware) affected the network systems of six hospital systems from New York to California over 24 hours. A few hospitals self-reported IT outages due to ransomware during that time. The attackers have demanded more than $1 million from unknown hospitals. According to the New York Times, the hackers are known to set the ransom at 10% of the organization's annual income. The federal government wants the hospital systems and healthcare providers to boost protection networks, ensure all the software updates are made, back up data, monitor access to their systems closely. Ryuk has been deployed as a payload from banking. Ryuk was first introduced in August 2018 as a derivative of Hermes 2.1 ransomware. One of the key reasons the attackers target healthcare organizations to get the monetary benefits in terms of ransom. In May 2017, National Health Services (NHS) in the UK were one of the victims of the ransomware attack. Almost 200,000 computers at 16 healthcare facilities affected by the WannaCry attack at that time. Thousands of patients were suffered from the outcomes of the attack as it stop down the many vital medical equipments [25].

2.1.3 Nebraska medicine in Omaha attack

In September 2020, Nebraska Medicine first reported the outage, and the health system anticipates its computer network will remain down. The adversary incident affected the Nebraska Medicine IT system and required many patient's appointments to be postponed or rescheduled. The attack also affected the EHRs and computer systems for several other Regional Health Services because Nebraska Medicine powers their EHRs. Also, from Feb. to May 2020, there are more than 46 hospitals and health systems that had patient information exposed in a security hole at Blackbaud, a company that stores donor information for organizations, including health systems [26].

2.1.4 DDoS attack at Boston's Children Hospital

Distributed Denial of Service (DDoS) occurs when the network is overloaded and it starts denial of availability to its recipients. There are a few times the DDoS attack happens unintentionally. But most of the time the cybercriminals created DDoS attack to get access the critical data, including the financial information of an organization. The healthcare system is one of the main targets for the hackers. In 2014, one of the most remarkable DDoS attacks targeted Boston's Children Hospital. The hospital system was attacked by DDoS when dealing with the case of parental withdrawal of a 14-year-old girl. The hospital had an about $300,000 loss to overcome the damage caused by the DDoS cyberattack [27].

2.1.5 Data breach at Montpellier University Hospital

Data breaches at the healthcare system have been rampant for the last decades as data breach is also a common types of cyberattacks. Almost all Attackers use phishing emails and manipulative web links to trick the user. The attacker will get access to the account as well as the network system when the user click on the suspicious web link receive in their email. On March 2019, the healthcare provider at the Montpellier University Medical Center found out that an outsider can access one of the employee email accounts. The employee of this medical center unintentionally clicked on a malicious link in the phishing email. As a result attacker got accessed in his/her account and as well as to the hospital network. Around 600 computers were affected due to this data breach [28]. The healthcare provider discovered that the affected account had sensitive patient information, including name, social security number, date of birth, insurance details, etc.

2.1.6 Internal threats

Besides external cybersecurity threats, healthcare providers sometimes have to face internal threats as well. These internal threats to the organizations are either due to human error or as a result of a breach of an employment contract. According to several case studies, there are three types of internal attacks: the carelessness/negligence of employee or contractor, the criminal or malicious insider, and the credential thief (imposter risk) [28].

2.2 Medjacking

Medjacking is the practice of attacking and manipulating a medical device and instrument with the intent to harm a patient. The malfunctioning of any medical instruments at hospital and/or clinic is very distressing and might have severe fatal consequences. The faulty diagnostic results from any medical instruments could lead to the wrong prescription. If any medical devices are not operating properly, it might cause harm to patients that lead to death, rather than help. Medjacking is often targeted, especially to harm influential personalities, and to damage the reputation of the healthcare organization. Artificial Intelligence (AI) can support and help to improve the security aspect of manipulating medical devices and instruments [28].

3. Artificial intelligence

3.1 How artificial intelligence helps in healthcare security and cybersecurity

Artificial intelligence (AI) can provide a device or software program the ability to interpret complex data, including images, video text, and speech, or other sounds and to work on that interpretation to achieve the goal. Since AI-driven computers are programmed to make decisions with little human intervention, some wonder if machines will soon make the difficult decisions we now entrust to our doctors. It is important to separate fact from science fiction, because AI is already here and it is fundamentally changing medicine, according to David B. Agus, MD, a professor of medicine and engineering at the University of Southern California Keck School of Medicine and Viterbi School of Engineering.

AI has been employed in applications in various domains of healthcare including cancer research, cardiology, diabetes, mental health, identification of Alzheimer's disease, stroke-related studies, identification of cardiovascular disease, etc. Rather than robotics, AI in healthcare mainly refers to doctors and hospitals accessing vast data sets of potentially life-saving information. The recent advancement of computing power can analyze the different features from the multisensory data for predictive analytics to identify the potential health outcomes through the machine learning techniques. The artificial intelligence and machine learning techniques use statistical methods to analyze incoming sensory and network data to identify patterns and security threat and make a decision with a minimum human interaction.

3.2 AI in mobile heath (m-Health)

Mobile health (m-Health) is the employment of smartphones and mobile devices with their communication to assist healthcare. M-Health comprises a combination of mobile devices, medical sensors, and smartphones. There is plenty of research that has shown that the application of AI in healthcare systems can significantly improve the security of patient health analysis. Like, the author in [29] proposed an AI-based smartphone application for predicting heart failures and alert the users. Currently, the researchers and healthcare providers are use and apply the simple methods for generating alerts in case of emergency. But, there are a high number of false alerts generated in the present methodology. The authors of this work used predictive models to avoid the impact of these false alerts. The proposed predictive models built based on the 44 months clinical data collected from 242 patients' smartphone who had experienced a heart failure at least once. In this work, the best predictive model developed using an application of a Naïve Bayes Classifier based on integration of observing data and a set of questions from the various alerts. The author claimed that their proposed model can lower the yearly rate of false alerts for a heart patient from 28.64 to 7.8 gradually.

Another m-Health based approach for speech recognition of users who are affected with dysarthria proposed in [30]. In this work, the author showed that their approach can assist in the process of voice message generation. The Hidden Markov Model approach was employed to measure the overall proximity of a word used in a speech model and is personalized for a particular user. The Hidden Markov Models are used to build AI to estimate the unknown parameters in a mobile target moving in a define environment. The speech recognition accuracy of their methodology is only 67% based on the real life study of nine test subjects. The authors of this work showed that the difficulties in the process of communication with users decreased significantly by using their proposed technology compared to the already available methods in the market. The drawback of this approach is the lower accuracy in speech recognition hardware and need usual aid for the voice-output communication.

3.3 Internet of Things (IoT) and Cyber-Physical System (CPS) in the era of AI

Healthcare systems in hospitals/clinics are one of the key targets of attackers for carrying out Internet-of-Things (IoT) and Cyber-physical System (CPS)-focused cyberattacks. The most critical endpoints from the hospital security viewpoint are

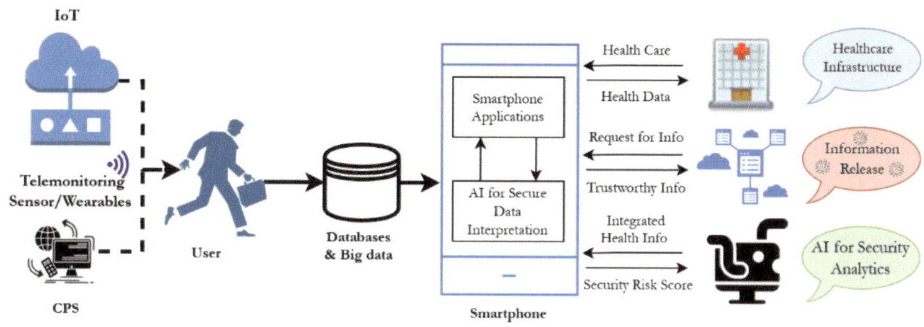

Figure 3.
AI for Smart m-Health (the workflow with IoT and CPS communicate with a smartphone via Wi-Fi or Bluetooth).

patient health monitoring, ventilation, anesthesia, infusion pumps, etc. There is increasing use of IoT in healthcare settings, including mobile devices, wearables, robots, drones, and contactless devices. IoT is enabling the control of coronavirus.

Early detection of Covid-19, isolation of infected people, and tracing possible contacts are critical to stopping the spread of the virus. IoT and CPS protocols, GPS, and Wi-Fi are providing solutions to the challenges that distance and accessibility would have posed. Using the IoT to fight virus outbreaks has been effective during Covid-19. Interconnected tech devices, such as smart thermometers to test a patient's temperature, are used to build up detailed datasets for more accurate analysis and diagnosis. Quarantine compliance is also greatly assisted by the use of IoT. By using a patient's existing smartphone or wearable devices, it is easier to ensure compliance with quarantine rules and establish patterns via track-and-trace methods.

A Cyber-Physical System (CPS) is a collection of sensors/devices interacting with each other and communicating with the physical world. Many CPS application is based on the medical devices used in smart healthcare technology. Advances in CPS will enable capability, adaptability, scalability, resiliency, safety, security, and useability that will expand the horizon of critical application in the healthcare system with cybersecurity. The ideas in CPS-based research are being challenged by the new research concepts emerging from AI and machine learning. The integration of AI with CPS especially with real-time secure health care operation creates new research opportunities with major societal implications. The application of AI and smart m-Health with the workflow including IoT and CPS communicate with a smartphone via Bluetooth or Wi-Fi is shown in **Figure 3**.

4. Cybersecurity

4.1 Cybersecurity for AI

Artificial Intelligence (AI) and machine learning are playing an important role in cybersecurity. AI-based cybersecurity systems can provide a clear knowledge of global and healthcare industry security threats to help make critically important decisions in a critical situation. AI techniques are expected to enhance cybersecurity by assisting human system managers with automated monitoring, analysis, and responses to adversarial attacks.

The research outcomes from the integrated AI and cybersecurity can lead to an extensive change in the understanding of the basis of cybersecurity. Also, this integrated results can help to motivate and educate healthcare providers about cybersecurity in the age of AI in an innovative way. Fundamental research in AI together with cybersecurity research might expand existing AI opportunities and resources in cybersecurity analytics and workforce development. AI relies on innovations like Machine Learning, Deep Learning, Natural Language Processing, and so forth to make it hard for malicious actors to access servers and other important data. AI has crossed many milestones and now it is turning towards cybersecurity. According to MIT, AI can detect about 85% of cyberattacks and help to secure IoT and CPS systems including the healthcare industry from cyberattacks. The prototype AI-based cybersecurity system is shown in **Figure 4**.

AI, Machine Learning (ML), and Deep Learning (DL) are overlapping and someone can easily get confused with these terminologies. The AI technique can help computers to mimic human behavior. The machine learning is a subset of AI, which give computers to automatically learn models and representation of the data sets. The deep learning is a subset of machine learning that help computers to solve multi-layer neural network complex problems. Use AI and leveraging machine learning and deep learning techniques are the smart choice to extract and analyze the sensory data from a smart IoT system. The researchers in [31] evaluate the performance of eleven famous ML and DL algorithms using six IoT related data sets. The authors of this paper showed that considering their performance evaluation matrics, including precision, recall, f1-score, accuracy, execution time, area under receiver operating characteristic curve (ROC-AUC) score, and confusion matrix, Random Forest performed better than other ML models. Also, they showed that ANN and CNN have interesting results comparing with other deep learning models.

4.2 How AI is helpful in cybersecurity

AI is changing the game for cybersecurity, analyzing massive data sets to improve response times and augment under-resourced security operations. AI and machine learning are playing a key role in cybersecurity to identify potential threats. AI can use to remove noise as well as unwanted data from any signals or data sets. Also, currently most of the security experts utilize AI to understand the cyber environment.

4.2.1 Network security

For network security in the healthcare system, AI can confidently navigate HIPAA privacy law and prevent patient data from wearable devices or public system from ending up in the hands of unauthorized personnel. The three important ways to use AI for network security are to use machine learning to detect

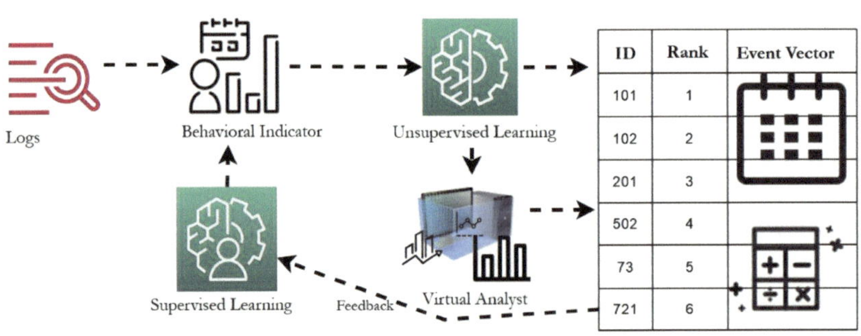

Figure 4.
AI-based Cybersecurity System.

AI-based cyberthreats, use AI to enhance human judgment, and use AI as a tool to save security policy and network architecture. AI can detect new threats based on the identification and analysis of threats before they exploit vulnerabilities in the network. Also, a human can become complacent and reliant on AI and machine learning to handle the cybersecurity of their network.

4.2.2 Faster response times

A key benefit of AI in cybersecurity is AI can immediately identify any anomalous behavior and suspected problems and prevent the healthcare systems from a potential cyber threat. The ability to detect a threat and respond to it quickly can improve the security system of any organization that costs resources and reputation. Three important strategies to improve detection and response before threats damage a critical healthcare system are managed security service, getting ahead with AI, and centralizing the response. Managed security service providers offer outsourced monitoring of security devices and systems. The cyberattack and ransomware attacks lead the healthcare industry to use AI to better and faster detect threats by recognizing patterns and anomalies. Centralization is very important as most of the healthcare industry faces a lack of centralization when dealing with a cyberattack. Human digital security specialists will even now make the approaches the needs of the episodes to be taken care of. However, it can be additionally helped by AI frameworks that consequently recommend plans for improving reactions.

4.2.3 Phishing detection and prevention

Phishing attacks are one of the most common security challenges for an individual and a company in keeping their information secure, where malicious actors attempt to convey their payload utilizing a phishing assault. AI and machine learning may assume a noteworthy job in forestalling and deflecting phishing assaults. Computer-based intelligence machine learning can recognize and follow over 10,000 dynamic phishing sources. Additionally, AI-machine learning works at filtering phishing dangers from everywhere throughout the world. Phishing attacks can have several different goals, including malware delivery, stealing money, and credential theft. Most phishing scams are designed to steal personal information. There is no limitation in its comprehension of phishing efforts to a particular geological territory. Computer-based intelligence has made it conceivable to separate between a phony site and a real one rapidly.

4.2.4 Secure authentication

Security provisioning or authentication has become a key issue in wireless networks due to their vital roles in supporting numerous services. The Physically recognizable proof in which AI used to explore the various security elements to distinguish a user could be the primary way to security verification. A smartphone can utilize the scanner for unique fingerprint and facial expression to permit for a secure login of a user. The smartphone application examines the fingerprint and facial expression to identify if the login is true. Also, AI technique can investigate the different features to verify the user authentication and allow the user to access information from any device.

4.2.5 Behavioral analytics

One of the important uses of AI in cybersecurity originates from its ability to analyze behavior. This means the machine learning calculations can learn and make an example of your conduct by breaking down how you utilize your gadget and online stages. The use of AI in healthcare like DNA/genome research is truly captivating to read. People are involved in the behavior part of cybersecurity. Also, machine behavior plays a significant role in cyber events. AI is changing our lifestyle, including the way we live, work, and play. With more and more healthcare data being collected from multisensory system and medical instruments and being processed, predict and behavioral analytics allow to generate insight and take a necessary action.

In conclusion, AI techniques have experienced quick change and progress from being inconsequential specialized. This will help cybersecurity specialists in managing moves identified with the discovery and avoidance of cyberattacks. AI can help to detect cybersecurity dangers and advise the specialists to take proper actions. The job of AI is expanding different parts of data innovation like AI in Cybersecurity, Software Testing, and Data Security.

5. Challenges in intelligent cybersecurity

Cybersecurity is the main concern of the nation's overall cyber-physical security and economic interests. The security analysts in every organization are facing many challenges related to cybersecurity including securing federal and state confidential data. One needs to distinguish between the immediate goals and long-term goals when coming up with the long-term analysis, development, and application of AI in cybersecurity. There are a variety of ways AI can be directly applied in cybersecurity. Currently, there are immediate cybersecurity issues that need a lot of intelligent solutions. In the future, users will see the promising views of the application of fully new principles of data handling. A key application space of AI is the data management for cyber threats. AI-based systems are already getting used in several applications, like the security measures hidden within the software. However, AI will get a wider application as massive databases for healthcare systems are developed. Many technologies are usually mentioned as most of the healthcare databases are incorporating AI for cybersecurity. However, there are many different technologies that, if they reach a high level of sophistication, would bring about the creation of smarter-than-human intelligence.

6. How to improve cybersecurity for AI

The development of AI and machine learning technologies will impact cybersecurity in several ways. Cyber attackers can attack any network systems from anywhere in the world, at any time. It is noticed that cybersecurity applications have received massive technological advancement over the last few years. There are many ways to improve cybersecurity for AI, like improving cyber threat detection with machine learning, AI and machine learning plays an important role in mitigating phishing attacks, automated network security, robust behavioral analytics, etc. AI and machine learning make smarter cybersecurity possible and these emerging technologies have vast potential applications in healthcare, finance, retail, etc. There are several similar issues to deal with the question of how AI systems are secure when they are used to augment the security of the collected healthcare data and computer networks. The application of AI security solutions to respond to quickly evolving threats makes the need to secure AI itself even more pressing. It is all the more important that those algorithms be protected from interference, compromise, or misuse if we rely on machine learning algorithms to detect and protect from cyberattacks. Increasing dependence on AI for critical functions and services will not only create greater incentives for attackers to target those algorithms, but also the potential for each successful attack to have more severe consequences.

The improvement of cybersecurity and safety for AI is one of the key challenges. The US Government has already indicated their interest in cybersecurity targeting certain types of technology, including the IoT, CPS, and voting systems. Recently, AI has become more popular and widely used technology in many different sectors including the healthcare industry. The policymakers find it increasingly necessary to consider the intersection of cybersecurity with AI. Recently, several researchers working on to reduce the possibility for adversaries to access confidential AI training data or models in healthcare systems during the era of Covid-19.

As mentioned above, one of the key security threats to AI systems is the possibility for adversaries to compromise the integrity of their decision-making processes. The way to achieve this when adversaries take the direct control of an AI system so that they can decide the outputs the system generates and the decisions it makes. An attacker might try to influence those decisions directly by delivering malicious inputs or training data to an AI model.

7. Mathematical modeling for healthcare and cybersecurity

Mathematics is one of the key components for cybersecurity data analysis. Mathematics has a direct impact on the advancement of the science of cybersecurity. Considering the complexity and dynamics of cyberspace it is essential to have a formal scientific basis for the field of cybersecurity. Mathematics plays a critical role in the construction of the science of cybersecurity.

There have been many research studies for modeling of dynamics and spread of COVID-19. Most of them are based on the Susceptible (S_i)-Exposed (E_i)-Infected (I_i)-Removed (R_i) and susceptible-infected-recovered (SIR) model as shown in **Figure 5**. Susceptible individuals might acquire the infection at a given rate when they are in contact with an infectious individual and enter the exposed disease state before they become infectious and later either recover or die.

For a given age group i, epidemic transitions can be described as,

$$S_{i,t+1} = S_{i,t} - \beta\, S_{i,t} \sum_{j=1}^{n} C_{i,j} I^{c}_{j,t} - \alpha\, \beta_{i,t} \sum_{j=1}^{n} C_{i,j} I^{sc}_{j,t} \tag{1}$$

$$E_{i,t+1} = (1-k) E_{i,t} + \beta\, S_{i,t} \sum_{j=1}^{n} C_{i,j} I^{c}_{j,t} + \alpha\beta\, S_{i,t} \sum_{j=1}^{n} C_{i,j} I^{sc}_{j,t} \tag{2}$$

$$I_{j,t+1} - \rho_i k\, E_{i,t} + (1-\gamma) I^{c}_{j,t} \tag{3}$$

$$I_{j,t+1} = (1-\rho_i) k\, E_{i,t} + (1-\gamma) I^{c}_{j,t} \tag{4}$$

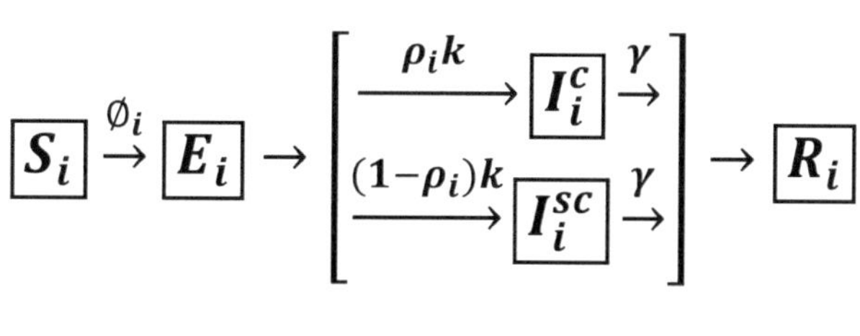

Figure 5
SEIR model for Dynamics and Spread Prediction of Covid-19 [32].

$$R_{i,t+1} = R_{i,t} + \gamma I^{c}_{j,t+1} + \gamma I^{sc}_{j,t+1} \quad (5)$$

Where,

β = Transmission rate.

$C_{i,j}$ = Contact of age group j made by age group i.

$k = 1 - e^{-}\left(\frac{1}{d_L}\right)$ = the daily probability of an exposed individual becoming infectious.

$\gamma = 1 - e^{-}\left(\frac{1}{d_I}\right)$ = the daily probability that an infected individual recovers when the average duration of infection is dI.

d_L = average incubation period.

d_I = average duration of infection.

α = infection acquired from subclinical individual.

ρ_i = the probability that an individual is symptomatic or clinical.

$1 - \rho_i$ = probability of an infected case being asymptomatic or subclinical.

I^c = an infected individual can be clinical.

I^{sc} = an infected individual can be subclinical.

$\varnothing_{i,t} = \beta \sum_j C_{i,j} I^{c}_{j,t} + \alpha\beta \sum_j C_{i,j} I^{sc}_{j,t}$ =The force of infection.

Primarily, these models were used in the past for the research of epidemic spreading with various forms of networks of transmission. The principle of AI techniques, like, Neural Networks (NN) are based on the collection of artificial neurons, without any prior knowledge, this AI technique automatically generates identification characteristics for cybersecurity.

8. Carbon footprint (gCO_2eq) and Artificial Intelligence

AI is an important factor in our daily life and an important factor in the science of the healthcare system. Deep learning (a process by which computer models are trained to identify the patterns from a data set) training requires computationally intensive computers and a large amount of power and associated carbon emission. In a report published by researchers from the University of Massachusetts Amherst estimating the amount of power required for training certain type of Artificial Neural Network (ANN) architecture emits roughly 626, 000 pounds of carbon dioxide [33]. This will get more severe during the model development phase. The proposed deep neural networks are deployed on diverse hardware platforms with different computational properties.

Researchers from MIT-IBM Watson AI Lab introduced a novel AI system "Once-for-all network" with improved computational efficiency and with a smaller carbon footprint. In their approach, the system, train a large neural network comprising of many different sizes subnetworks and a large number of IoT devices connected to the network. All the subnetworks used in the system can be tailored to diverse hardware platforms without retrain them. In their work, the authors estimate that the computer-vision model process will require $\frac{1}{1300}$ the carbon emission compared to the existing neural architecture search approaches. Also, the approach reduces the interference time with a minimum of 1.5–2.6 times [33].

Another approach for tracking and predicting the energy and carbon footprint of training deep learning models is explained in [34]. The tool "Carbontracker" is used to report energy and carbon footpring alongside of performance metrics of model development and training. In this work, to predict the accuracy on reducing the carbon footprint, the authors experimentaly evaluate the tool on different convolutional neural network (CNN) architectures and healthcare data sets.

9. Future directions

Technology is changing continuously, and it is important to stay on the cutting edge. In the future, incorporating hybrid software would be a good idea to secure the health data. Cybersecurity experts should intelligently manage the system since AI and machine learning are still susceptible to attacks. It is recommended that in the future data governance and compliance strategies should be a top priority with more security and privacy legislation on the horizon. Many cybersecurity applications can be made easier and more efficiently with machine learning algorithms. In the future, this technology will lighten the weight of a heavy cybersecurity workload and will reduce human error.

That same reduction in human error is also applicable to health diagnoses. Medical errors, some of which are incorrect diagnoses, may result in approximately 251,000 deaths every year according to [35]. Additionally, many more die every year because they do not get treatment quickly enough. Healthcare systems that incorporate AI into the diagnosis process, as well as the smart health sector, could see a drop in these deaths due to the AI more accurately diagnosing a patient, as well as identifying the problem sooner.

10. Conclusion

Artificial Intelligence is fast, growing field with broad applications. Recent cybersecurity events that targeted healthcare systems have highlighted cybersecurity vulnerabilities that have compromised the confidentiality, integrity, and availability of data for the affected institutions. Further, these events have shown that even with care, it only takes one slip up to cost a business or organization millions of dollars and several years to resolve the issue. Additionally, the COVID-19 pandemic has shown the need for improvements in the healthcare sector that can make diagnoses more accurate and more efficient. One proposed approach is to integrate AI into both cybersecurity and healthcare. AI is already used in the medical field to diagnose many types of cancer, as well as many other illnesses. Further integration of AI into the smart health field can lead to quicker treatment, as well as make the diagnosis process more efficient. AI is also already finding use in the cybersecurity field to detect threats or to help aid experts in identifying and dealing with threats. Continued integration of AI in the cybersecurity field will lead to more refined, and robust systems that are capable of dealing with ever-changing cyber threats.

Acknowledgements

We would like to thank the Office of Sponsored Awards and Research Support at USC Upstate for the partial funding of this project under the grant no. UP000-981350-A001-101. We would also like to thank the anonymous reviewers for reviewing earlier drafts of this chapter.

Conflict of interest

The authors declare no conflict of interest regarding this chapter.

Author details

A.K.M. Jahangir Alam Majumder* and Charles B. Veilleux
Division of Mathematics and Computer Science, University of South Carolina Upstate, Spartanburg, SC, USA

*Address all correspondence to: majumder@mailbox.sc.edu

IntechOpen

© 2021 The Author(s). Licensee IntechOpen. This chapter is distributed under the terms of the Creative Commons Attribution License (http://creativecommons.org/licenses/by/3.0), which permits unrestricted use, distribution, and reproduction in any medium, provided the original work is properly cited.

References

[1] Healthcare Cybersecurity- the impact of AI, IoT-related threats and recommended approaches" by Richard Staynings, Chief Seurity Strategist, Cylera. September 18, 2019. https://www.healthcareitnews.com/news/asia-pacific/healthcare-cybersecurity-impact-ai-iot-related-threats-and-recommended-approaches.

[2] McGee, Timothy Matthew, "Evaluating The Cyber Security In The Internet Of Things: Smart Home Vulnerabilities" (2016). West Point ETD. 6. https://digitalcommons.usmalibrary.org/faculty_etd/6

[3] Jacob Rodrigues M, Postolache O, Cercas F. Physiological and Behavioral Monitoring Systems for Smart Healthcare Environments: A Review. Sensors (Basel). 2020 April 12; 20(8): 2186. Doi:10.3390/s20082186. PMID: 32290639; PMCID: PMC7218909.

[4] Gope P., and Hwang T., "BSN-Care: A Secure IoTBased Modern Healthcare System Using Body Sensor Network," IEEE Sensors Journal, vol. 16, no. 5, pp. 1368–1376, 2016.

[5] Zhu N., Diethe T., Camplani M., Tao L., Burrows A., Twomey N., Kaleshi D., Mirmehdi M., Flach P., and Craddock I., "Bridging e-Health and the Internet of Things: The SPHERE Project," IEEE Intelligent Systems, vol. 30, no. 4, pp. 39–46, 2015

[6] Majumder A. J., Dedmondt J. W., Jones S. and Asif A. A., "A Smart Cyber-Human System to Support Mental Well-Being through Social Engagement," *2020 IEEE 44th Annual Computers, Software, and Applications Conference (COMPSAC)*, Madrid, Spain, 2020, pp. 1050-1058, doi: 10.1109/COMPSAC48688.2020.0-134.

[7] Chang S. H., Chiang R. D., Wu S. J., and Chang W. T., "A Context-Aware, Interactive M-Health System for Diabetics," IT Professional, vol. 18, no. 3, pp. 14–22, 2016.

[8] Pasluosta C. F., Gassner H., Winkler J., Klucken J., and Eskofier B. M., "An emerging era in the management of Parkinson's disease: Wearable technologies and the internet of things," IEEE Journal of Biomedical and Health Informatics, vol. 19, no. 6, pp. 1873–1881, 2015.

[9] Arcadius T. C., Gao B., Tian G., and Yan Y., "Structural Health Monitoring Framework Based on Internet of Things: A Survey," IEEE Internet of Things Journal, vol. PP, no. 99, p. 1, 2017.

[10] Ahad A, Tahir M, Aman Sheikh M, Ahmed KI, Mughees A, Numani A. Technologies Trend towards 5G Network for Smart Health-Care Using IoT: A Review. Sensors (Basel). 2020;20 (14):4047. Published 2020 Jul 21. doi: 10.3390/s20144047

[11] 2019 Global Health Care Outlook Shaping the Future—Deloitte. [(accessed on 10 June 2020)]; Available online: https://www2.deloitte.com/content/dam/Deloitte/global/Documents/Life-Sciences-Health-Care/gx-lshc-hc-outlook-2019.pdf.

[12] Liu X., Jia M., Zhang X., Lu W. A novel multichannel Internet of things based on dynamic spectrum sharing in 5G communication. *IEEE Internet Things J.* 2018;**6**:5962–5970. doi: 10.1109/JIOT.2018.2847731.

[13] Li D. 5G and intelligence medicine—How the next generation of wireless technology will reconstruct healthcare? *Precis. Clin. Med.* 2019;**2**:205–208. doi: 10.1093/pcmedi/pbz020.

[14] Chen J, See KC "Artificial Intelligence for COVID-19: Rapid Review" J Med Internet Res 2020;22 (10):e21476

[15] Yassine HM, Shah Z. How could artificial intelligence aid in the fight against coronavirus? Expert Rev Anti Infect Ther 2020 Jun 29;18(6):493-497.

[16] Mashamba-Thompson TP, Crayton ED. Blockchain and Artificial Intelligence Technology for Novel Coronavirus Disease-19 Self-Testing. Diagnostics (Basel) 2020 Apr 01;10(4): 198.

[17] Institute of Medicine (US) Committee on Assuring the Health of the Public in the 21st Century. The Future of the Public's Health in the 21st Century. Washington (DC): National Academies Press (US); 2002. 5, The Health Care Delivery System. Available from: https://www.ncbi.nlm.nih.gov/books/NBK221227/

[18] National Science Foundation (NSF)- "Smart Health and Biomedical Research in the Era of AI and Advanced Data Science", https://www.nsf.gov/pubs/2021/nsf21530/nsf21530.htm

[19] Lin SH, Chen MY. [Artificial Intelligence in Smart Health: Investigation of Theory and Practice]. Hu Li Za Zhi. 2019 Apr;66(2):7-13. Chinese. doi: 10.6224/JN.201904_66 (2).02. PMID: 30924509.

[20] Gopal G, Suter-Crazzolara C, Toldo L, Eberhardt W. Digital transformation in healthcare - architectures of present and future information technologies. Clin Chem Lab Med. 2019 Feb 25;57(3):328-335. doi: 10.1515/cclm-2018-0658. PMID: 30530878.

[21] Kamel Boulos MN, Peng G, VoPham T. An overview of GeoAI applications in health and healthcare. Int J Health Geogr. 2019 May 2;18(1):7. doi: 10.1186/s12942-019-0171-2. PMID: 31043176; PMCID: PMC6495523.

[22] Jeffery S., "Healthcare Cybersecurity in the Age of Covid-19: A Once-in-a-Lifetime Level of Distraction." Disaster Recovery Journal, November 2020.

[23] Zeina R., Marco A., Abdel-Badeeh S., "Machine Learning Approaches in Smart Health" 8th International Congress of Information and Communication Technology, ICICT 2019. Procedia Computer Science 154 (2019) 361–368.

[24] The University of Vermont (UVM) Health Network Cyberattack. https://www.uvmhealth.org/uvm-health-network-cyber-attack

[25] "Six hospital ransomware attacks in 24 hours prompts US advisory: 8 things to know" Laura Dyrda (Twitter) - Thursday, October 29th, 2020

[26] Nebraska Medicine reverts to paper records during computer network outage: 4 details. Laura Dyrda (Twitter) - Tuesday, September 22nd, 2020

[27] DDoS Case Study: Boston's Children's Hospital DDoS attack Mitigation. https://www.radware.com/security/ddos-experts-insider/ert-case-studies/boston-childrens-hospital-ddos-mitigation-case-study/ Cybersecurity & Healthcare During COVID-19

[28] Cybersecurity and Healthcare During Covid-19 by Susan Alexandra on April 2020.

[29] Larburu, N., Artetxe, A., Escolar, V., Lozano, A., and Kerexeta, J. "Artificial intelligence to prevent mobile heart failure patients decompensation in real time: monitoringbased predictive model," Mobile Information Systems, vol. 2018, Article ID 1546210, 11 pages, 2018.

[30] Hawley, M. S., Cunningham, S. P., Green, P. D. et al., "A voiceinput voice-output communication aid for people with severe speech impairment," IEEE Transactions on Neural Systems and

Rehabilitation Engineering, vol. 21, no. 1, pp. 23–31, 2013.

[31] Vakili, M., Ghamsari, M., & Rezaei, M. (2020). Performance Analysis and Comparison of Machine and Deep Learning Algorithms for IoT Data Classification. arXiv preprint arXiv: 2001.09636.

[32] Kiesha P., Yang L., Timothy W. R., Adam J. K., Rosalind M. E., Nicholas D., "The effect of control strategies to reduce social mixing on outcomes of the COVID-19 epidemic in Wuhan, China: a modelling study," Centre for the Mathematical Modelling of Infectious Diseases COVID-19 Working Group. March 25, 2020.

[33] https://news.mit.edu/2020/artificial-intelligence-ai-carbon-footprint-0423.

[34] Lasse F., Benjamin K., Raghavendra S., "Carbontracker: Tracking and Predicting the Carbon Footprint of Training Deep Learning Models" ICML Workshop on "Challenges in Deploying and monitoring Machine Learning Systems", 2020.

[35] Anderson JG, Abrahamson K. Your Health Care May Kill You: Medical Errors. Stud Health Technol Inform. 2017;234:13-17. PMID: 28186008.

Chapter 5

Risk in Healthcare Information Technology: Creating a Standardized Risk Assessment Framework

Suzanna Schmeelk

Abstract

Data breaches are occurring at an unprecedented rate. Between June 2019 and early October 2020, over 564 data breaches affected over 36.6 million patients as posted to the United States Federal government HITECH portal. These patients are at risk for having their identities stolen or sold on alternative marketplaces. Some healthcare entities are working to manage privacy and security risks to their operations, research, and patients. However, many have some procedures and policies in place, with few (if any) centrally managing all their infrastructure risks. For example, many healthcare organizations are not tracking or updating all the known and potential concerns and elements into a centralized repository following industry best practice timetables for auditing and insurance quantification. This chapter examines known and potential problems in healthcare information technology and discusses a new open source risk management standardized framework library to improve the coordination and communication of the aforementioned problematic management components. The healthcare industry would benefit from adopting such a standardized risk-centric framework.

Keywords: risk associated with computer communications, healthcare, data breaches, GDPR, HITECH, HIPAA, standardized risk library, risk management, patient information, identity theft, cybersecurity, laws, penetration test, risk assessments, insurance

1. Introduction

Across the globe, data security is becoming more regulated. For example, in the European Union, the General Data Protection Regulation (GDPR) protects its citizens [1]. In China, the Cybersecurity Law of 2017 was one of the first well known laws passed to protect the data and communications of its citizens [2]. In the United States of America, medical entities in the country's critical infrastructure are covered under Federal laws to protect patient information. Specifically, the Health Insurance Portability and Accountability Act (HIPAA) [3] and Health Information Technology for Economic and Clinical Health Act (HITECH) [4] are Federal-level regulations for covered entities that secure patient-protected health information (PHI). PHI covers a gamut of different identifiers and includes patient names, birthdays, social security numbers, medical record numbers, license plate numbers, biometric data, among a few others. The digital form of PHI is electronic PHI or ePHI. In the United States, vendors and services which are not covered under HIPAA (perhaps because they do not bill patients for services rendered) are regulated by the Federal Trade Commission (FTC) and must self-report health data breaches to the FTC [5]. Furthermore, the European Commission officially ratified the final version of the GDPR to include notification from a breached supervisory authority to be made within 72 hours (or provide reasons for a delay) [1].

In the United States, both HIPAA-covered and non-covered entities may also be under other legal requirements, such as non-disclosure, confidentiality restrictions, or other security requirements, for other organizational, research, or employee data.

The management within covered groups has historically remained siloed intra-organization where different components of the organizational risk are being managed and decisions made by different units within the organizations without a standardized and well-connected systematic methodology. For example, the legal, audit, budget, health informatics, security, privacy, medical, and information systems teams may all be disjointly managed, causing frustrations in adequately quantifying and coordinating the organizational risks. In such disjoint cases, an exception to an organizational policy may result in unidentified operational risk if the different departments are not consistently coordinated and periodically reviewing, perhaps updating, the associated risks.

This chapter begins by describing data breach risks in HIPAA-covered entities as reported to the United States government that cause patients higher risks for identity theft. Then it integrates current research into building a standardized risk assessment library that enables both inter- and intra-organizational risk coordination. This design facilitates standardizing and communicating risks as well as reasonable internal statistics related to technical and administrative limitations, organizational policy exceptions, and federal legal requirements to inform the business, auditors, insurance companies, and business associates of risks.

2. Patient information data breaches can lead to patient identity theft

In the United States, citizens are protected by federal, state, and potentially smaller sub-state regulations. Each industry sector are potentially under unique legal and other sector-specific requirements. In fact, today most, if not all, states have different personally identifying information (PII) legislation. Historically, these laws are not well understood and are written in most cases by non-technical writers. As such, the legal and technical specifications have gaps both in understanding and in the feasibility of current technological constraints.

2.1 Entities covered under HIPAA

HIPAA requires at least three covered groups, referred to by the law as Covered Entities, to protect health information. Examples of covered entities are: healthcare providers, health Plans, and business associates. Healthcare providers transmit electronic patient information in connection with a Health and Human Services (HHS)-adopted standard transaction. Health plans include insurance companies, health maintenance organizations (HMOs), corporate health plans, and government programs. Business associates are external groups/organizations that perform activities or services on ePHI on behalf of another group covered

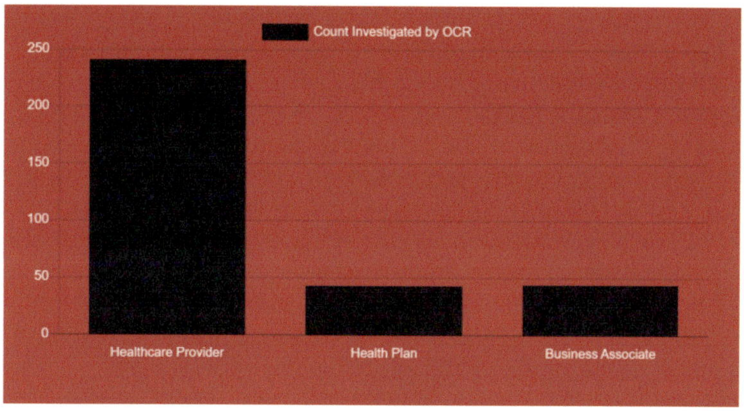

Figure 1.
OCR-covered entities investigated.

under HIPAA. **Figure 1** [6] shows one year of reports by covered entity to the Office of Civil Rights (OCR).

2.2 Risks in HIPAA-covered entities

Research at large has studied risk management of medical information [7–10], but not specifically as related by different HIPAA-covered domains. Recent research [6, 7, 11] explores potential concerns for each legally covered segment based on self-report to the US Government as required by the HITECH Act. In the sector-specific threat probability-specific research [6, 7, 11] over a one-year interval, the research showed that different the different domains may indeed have different sources of concerns and issues. For example, healthcare providers and business associates have reportedly different higher probability of concerns to alleviate than health plan entities, as shown in **Figure 2** [6]. This indicates that the different domains may need to manage their threats differently by perhaps investing more heavily in different mitigating controls.

2.3 Data breaches reported to the HHS OCR across the USA

The HHS unauthorized data release portal provides the number of affected individuals from the cybersecurity events for each self-reported or discovered data release. **Figure 3** [6] shows states across the USA with the most reported individuals, whom are now at risk from the leaking of their patient data. In any given

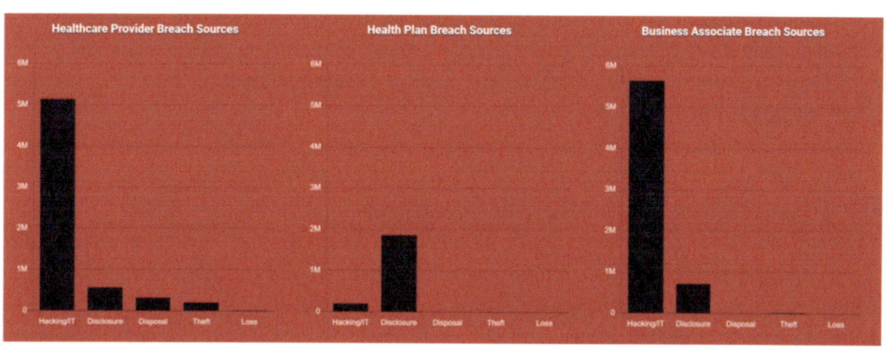

Figure 2.
OCR-covered entities risk sources.

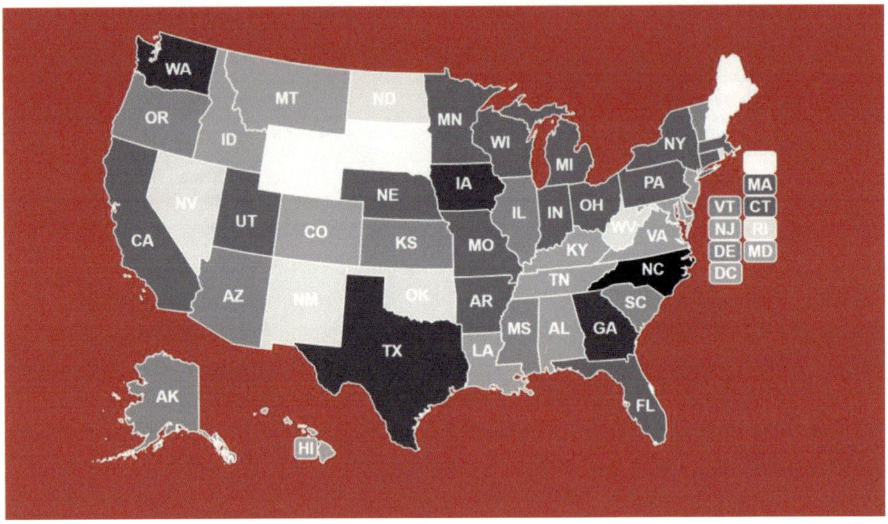

Figure 3.
OCR breached individuals by state.

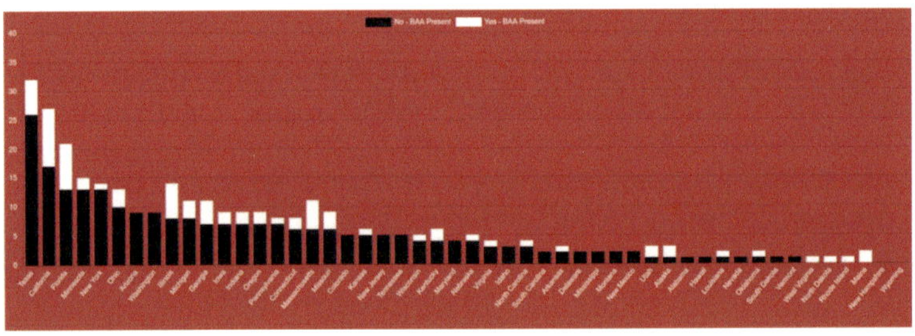

Figure 4.
OCR-covered entities investigated BAA by state.

one-year interval, each state may be equally likely to have higher counts depending on the released data size. Further research is needed to determine state likelihood.

2.4 Reported data breach counts per state sorted by number of reports

Another element tracked on the HHS portal is the presence of business associate agreements (BAA). A provider enters into a BAA with an outside party when an outside party receives access to the provider's ePHI. A properly written BAA somewhat "protects" the provider if the outside party breaches the ePHI. **Figure 4** [6] shows state BAA presence notated with by the HHS portal with either a "yes" or "no." The portal reports are not described, so the research below shows the categorical data as posted to the portal.

3. Risk assessment literature and standards

Risk management has been slowly moving into industry. In the United States, HIPAA mandates risk assessment be in place prior to new technology's being integrated into an organization.

Recently, in October 2020, Eddy and Perlrotha [12] reported on a cyber-attack that resulted in a patient death. The attack occurred when "ransomware invaded

DOI: http://dx.doi.org/10.5772/intechopen.96456

30 servers at University Hospital Düsseldorf [,...] crashing systems and forcing the hospital to turn away emergency patients." This is one of the first ransomware-attack-related suspected deaths reported publicly. In such a high-profile and morbid case, we can see the essential importance for having a standardized language for discussing cyber-risks.

3.1 Risk assessment standards

The United States National Institute of Standards and Technologies (NIST) has produced many Special Publications on Risk Assessments [13]. **Figures 5** and **6** [14] show NIST's generic risk model and risk assessment process respectively. In fact, many organizations around the world are following the NIST Risk Assessment frameworks.

3.2 Automating risk assessments

Risk assessment automation has been proposed in the form of automated penetration testing frameworks [9–11, 13–19]. Testing frameworks and automated tools are extremely useful for detecting known bugs and vulnerabilities. However, in general, these tools do not report on the larger risk-assessment picture. Specifically, they may not accurately report on legal requirements or help an organization prepare for prospective data-breach-associated costs. In addition, there is limited (if any) language standardization on risk findings to enable intra- and inter-organizational risk communication, which is essential for subsequent auditing and legal ramifications.

3.3 Framework libraries for malware and software developments

In addition to developing a standardized framework, NIST and MITRE.org have worked tirelessly to produce a standardized dictionary for attack and malware. For example, they have produced the *Common Attack Pattern Enumeration and Classification (CAPEC)* [20] to classify attacks. NIST maintains the *National Vulnerability Database (NVD)* [21] to identify products with well-known vulnerabilities. In addition to attacks, these organizations are iteratively developing vulnerability dictionaries. For example, MITER sponsors the *Common Weakness Enumeration (CWE)* [22] and NIST sponsors the *Bug Framework (BF)* [23, 24]). These standardized frameworks are purposefully agnostic to vendors, languages, and industry sectors. They have been instrumental and essential for industry, government, and

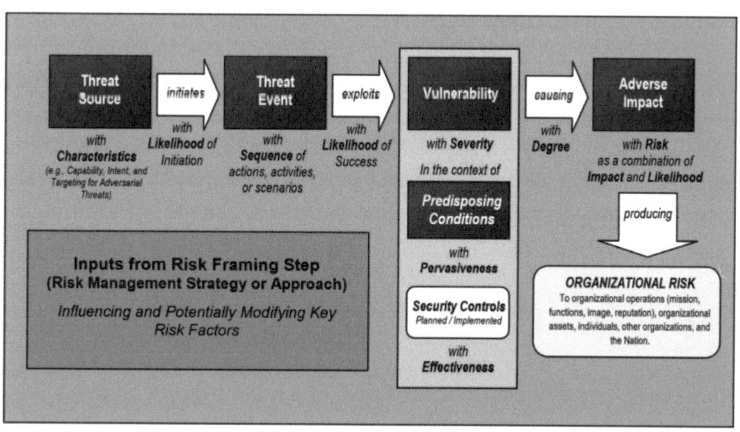

Figure 5.
NIST's generic risk model with key risk factors.

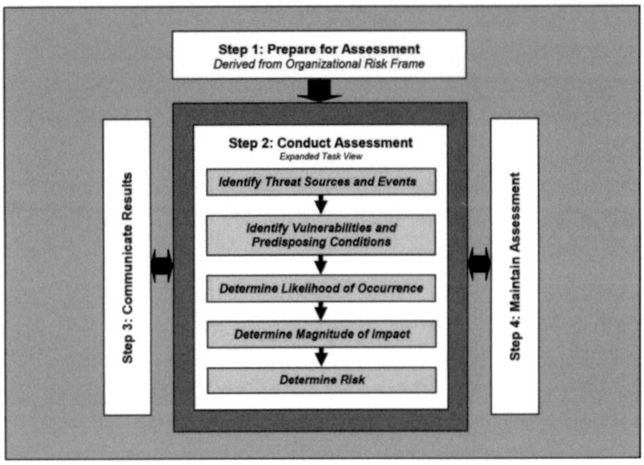

Figure 6.
NIST risk assessment process.

academia to discuss and communicate software vulnerabilities, assurances, and development techniques. As humans need a standard spoken dictionary to communicate with each other on day-to-day activities, so do they need a similar dictionary to discuss technical activities.

3.4 Penetration testing reports

As risk management is still clearly its own type of innovation phase within the technology adoption life-cycle, risk researchers are finding a need to communicate risk through standardized language. For example, let us consider a penetration test report. Historically, there is none of the following: (1) a fixed template, (2) a fixed-strategy, or (3) fixed-finding language. Such non-standardization is subject to extreme bias and misrepresentation. In fact, if every internal or external penetration test is written differently, how can any organization fully understand their own risks? Similarly, if every employee in an organization spoke their own verbal language, how could anything be communicated? Historically, industry has focused on standardizing software vulnerabilities and malicious code patterns. A major gap still exists for risk management components, including budgeting for financial penalties and legal ramifications.

3.5 Risk assessment education

Research on risk-assessment education has primarily focused on learning penetration testing techniques [25]. The curriculums discussed in this research neither considers the meta-organizational risk nor risks specifically associated with the medical sector. Schmeelk [26] fills a literature gap by emphasizing that all the risk components should be strategically aligned in terms of standardization.

4. Risk assessment library considerations

Managing the risk in a medical setting is unique because of specific regulations that come with significant potential financial fines and corrective actions. For example, outside and inside risk management strategies may not properly align. Also, many organizations, especially in healthcare, are employing a task-based ticketing system to track internal processes. These ticketing systems enable the Information

System silos and other organizational risk components to entirely misalign and improperly manage risk by using neither standardized nor repeatable language.

Schmeelk [26] reports that the following five subsections should be included in identifying organizational components. As a centralized library has yet to be created, a working group should focus on exactly what to include in a standardized public-risk-assessment language dictionary. Important historical components are: legal, training, vendor, and system security requirements, as well as organizational controls. A standardized risk-finding library encourages cross-organizational collaboration, communication, auditing, and legal consistency if a case ever goes to court.

4.1 Regulatory requirements

Regulatory requirements encompass a wide range of organizational responsibilities, which can be actual governmental laws and/or industry-specific requirements. Let us discuss both.

4.1.1 Industry-specific regulations

In the United States, medical critical infrastructure entities have both sector-specific regulatory requirements as well as other requirements, such as Payment Card Industry (PCI)-compliance, to consider in risk management [27]. If an organization does not pass PCI (re)compliance auditing, then they are at risk of losing the use of credit cards, among other payment sources under PCI regulations. In the past, organizations would consider themselves a cash-only facility if they lost PCI (re)compliance. Today, with the birth of cryptocurrencies and alternative payment methods not under PCI, losing the use of credit cards might not be as drastic as it has been historically. Other regulations include compliance with those from the International Standards Organization (ISO). Globally, there are many industry-specific regulations that are not necessarily enforceable laws.

4.1.2 Industry-specific Laws

Medical-covered entities under HIPAA/HITECH are subject to audits by the United States Health and Human Services (HHS) Office of Civil Rights (OCR). The OCR manages many civil rights across the United States in addition to HIPAA. Organizational breaches of patient electronic health information of over 500 individuals must be reported to the OCR as ruled in HITECH. Such breaches are both subject to federal fines and corrective actions. The OCR also can audit covered entities at any point in time. HIPAA is a very well-organized law. It has specific mandates for electronic health data requirements, which should be consistently mapped during a risk assessment to appropriately manage organizational risk. HHS lists many documents for guidance on their website, including mappings between NIST frameworks for cybersecurity and HIPAA requirements. These are extremely useful resources for practitioners.

4.2 Training requirements

Security education and training awareness (SETA) needs may occur at the vendor level or as federal, state, or city regulations. They are not only legally mandated in many instances for legal responsibilities, but also are ethical mitigations. For example, employing staff who have not been properly trained on data security and then holding them responsible for data security mistakes is unethical. In fact, in such a case, labor laws may also be violated. Also, in New York State, the loss of employee Social Security Numbers (SSN) through any sort of data breach is a crime subject to legal penalties [28].

4.2.1 Regulation trainings

Different regulations require different levels of SETA. In the credit card industry, organizations using alternatives to cash which are highly-corporately regulated must protect the data by complying with the Payment Card Industry (PCI) regulation. The PCI Data Security Standard (DSS) requires software developers for services using credit cards to be properly trained to code such systems. In addition, federal laws such as HIPAA also have specific training requirements. Lastly, little work on cybersecurity training is being done at state or city levels; however, proper awareness could be suddenly mandated at these local levels. If an organization or their accepted vendors are missing any of these training requirements, the organization may be financially liable.

4.2.2 Best practice trainings

Training based on current best practices is hard to assess because best practices in cybersecurity mean different things to different people and organizations. Training based on best practices is really subjective. Typically in the USA, organizations follow NIST and the Open Web Application Security Project (OWASP) guidance [14, 29]; however, still no industry-wide standards exist for exactly what best practices entail.

4.3 Service provider requirements

Service providers and vendors may be subject to different potential cybersecurity risk requirements than the actual provider or covered entity. If a covered entity works with a service provider, it should have proper agreements and risk mitigations in place. Two major sources of such agreements are: business associate agreements (BAAs) and other agreements, such as non-disclosure agreements. Let us examine both in the following subsections.

4.3.1 Business associate agreements (BAAs)

Historically, services providers (or business associates) working with a covered entity's sensitive patient data should have properly formed BAAs in place prior to releasing sensitive data or have a well-formed written legal justification as to why no such BAAs exist. Many HIPAA-covered entities still report breaches where a properly formed BAA was not in place. In such cases, all parties may be considered responsible for the breach by the HHS OCR in the USA.

4.3.2 Non-disclosure agreements and/or other agreements

Business partners may negotiate many different types of agreements and/or partner requirements for their data and products. One popular agreement in healthcare and healthcare research is non-disclosure agreements (NDA). Such agreements require parties not to release information without prior approval. In such a case, malware that makes NDA-protected data public by releasing it on a popular web application du jour, as well as its actual authors, could be faulted to violate the NDA. Cases that fall into this category can have many different negative outcomes, such as legal ramifications, reputational damage, among others.

In addition to NDAs, other Federal or organizational legal regulations may require risk assessments and other services or service-level agreements (SLAs). Similarly, the GDPR requires entities exposed to unauthorized access to notify affected breached individuals within a short timeframe. Violations to such agreements can have extremely negative consequences to the healthcare entities.

4.4 Application and system requirements

Application and system security are typically measured through certifications (e.g., International Organization for Standardization or other sources) or from internal tests prior to product release. HIPAA requires security assessments for systems and applications managing ePHI. Organizations can either develop their own methodologies to communicate risk that are acceptable by covered entities, or the entities themselves can ask to perform such probability assessments for adverse events. When the covered entity is performing the assessment, they must carefully obtain legal authorization to do so in most cases. In general, Information System silos prevent considering a full-threat landscape for the technical component with the legal, budget, and business use cases. Additionally, digital assessments may be filed for HHS OCR audits into the Integrated Risk Management (IRM) system without updates to the overall business threat mitigations. Periodically, teams must carefully reassess and update the stored organizational predicted levels. In such cases, the assessments are more of a risk "impression" rather than an informed, reproducible, scientific informing on the true likelihood and impact of adverse events. **Figure** 7 [30] provides a high-level overview of different technical security controls reported by NIST. The following subsections identify eight subcategories potentially employed during a risk assessment.

4.4.1 Authentication

According to NIST [30], authentication is the process or action of proving or showing something to be valid. Specifically, "The authentication control provides the means of verifying the identity of a subject to ensure that a claimed identity is valid." The OWASP Application Testing Guide [31] currently gives ten best-practice tests to perform for authentication: "Testing for Credentials Transported over an Encrypted Channel, Testing for Default Credentials, Testing for Weak Lock Out Mechanism, Testing for Bypassing Authentication Schema, Testing for Vulnerable Remember Password, Testing for Browser Cache Weaknesses, Testing for Weak Password Policy, Testing for Weak Security Question Answer, Testing for Weak Password Change or Reset Functionalities, and Testing for Weaker Authentication in Alternative Channel." It is important to realize that any best-practice guide at-large lists *top* threats and vulnerabilities without perhaps listing *all* threats and vulnerabilities.

4.4.2 Session management

Session management is the data flow between endpoints—typically following a client and server model. A web session is a series of requests and response transactions created by a client after authentication. In most cases, the endpoints communicate with a special identifier to limit re-authentications. Current best practices in session management include session flags, random token generation, and timeout intervals. The OWASP Application Testing Guide [31] currently lists the following eight session management tests: "Testing for Session Management Schema, Testing for Cookies Attributes, Testing for Session Fixation, Testing

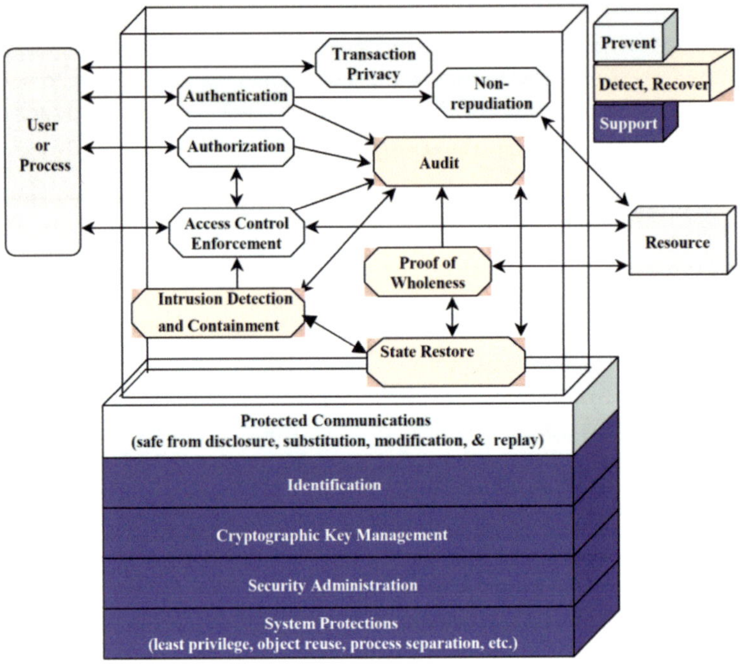

Figure 7.
Technical security controls.

for Exposed Session Variables, Testing for Cross Site Request Forgery, Testing for Logout Functionality, Testing Session Timeout, and Testing for Session Puzzling."

4.4.3 Data-in-transport, data-at-rest, data-in-use

The protection of sensitive information is fundamental to risk management. Data-in-motion is the transfer of material between endpoints. This category changes frequently and includes industry best practices in how to transmit the information, such as confidentiality controls and integrity controls during message transmission. Once information is stored on a system, it is referred to as data-at-rest. Lastly, data-in-use refers to messages in memory. Historically, a concern of data-in-use is that processes and other virtualized components could have improper access to the information.

4.4.4 Authorization and access control

Authorization policies define access capabilities for groups and entities. Access controls, sometimes referred to as permissions or privileges, are mitigating controls to enforce authorization. As such, access controls speak to lowering probabilities against unauthorized access, which could cause loss to data integrity, confidentiality, and availability. The effectiveness and the strength of unauthorized access reduction depend on the correctness of the admittance control decisions and the strength of entry control enforcement. The current OWASP Testing Framework [31] promotes the testing of four key elements in this security area: "Testing Directory Traversal File Include, Testing for Bypassing Authorization Schema, Testing for Privilege Escalation, Testing for Insecure Direct Object References."

4.4.5 Auditing and monitoring

Systems and applications should create records for auditing and monitoring. Specifically, archives should be generated before and after critical functions take place. These logs are stored in the system/server backend for regulatory requirements, performance indicators and other analytics. Different components are typically checked during risk management.

4.4.6 Injection and input vulnerabilities

Injections and input vulnerabilities enable maliciously crafted code to change the underlying intended behavior of a system or application. The OWASP Testing Guide [31] currently lists eighteen common best practice tests, including SQL/NoSQL injection, Cross Site Scripting (XSS), and HTTP injection attacks, among others.

4.5 Organizational control requirements

At the organizational-level, controls such as policies, procedures, physical security and financial budgeting should be considered during an assessment. However, these components of risk management can be managed by entirely different entities.

4.5.1 Policies and procedures

Organizations should have policies in place [32] at technical, physical, and administrative levels, which are repetitively and consistently followed to avoid different legal ramifications (e.g., from valid discrimination cases to data breaches). Standard operating procedures (SOPs) should also be in place and specifically in writing [32]. Specific procedures, which must be in place at the federal level, include business continuity and disaster recovery plans.

4.5.2 Physical and environmental security

This component describes the physical and environmental security aspects of the system, if any, which are requirements in the United States Federal HIPAA laws. Physical security encompasses the physical environment to lower the probability of a threat occurring in spaces such as public, private, and shared. It also includes ways to protect organizations from fire and other environmental concerns affecting risk.

4.5.3 Budget for adverse effects

Risk assessment traditionally includes developing a budget for adverse effects, such as in the Factor Analysis of Information Risk (FAIR) quantitative uncertainty analysis model. Many organizations are not storing-up financial resources in accordance with the uncertain probability being generated to pay for patient identity protections. Digital Guardian [33] has various reports on current costs per record; the costs vary with time. Simply indicating that a system is vulnerable to CSRF may really have no budgetary ramification under certain other conditions. Thus, probability of cost concerns inform on the overall organizational probability of concerns and insurance.

The HHS has historically been responsible for enforcing the Privacy and Security Rules of HIPAA [34]. For most HIPAA covered entities, the HHS OCR enforcement of the Privacy Rule began April 14, 2003, and the Security Rule began on April 20, 2005. The web portal currently lists government corrective action plans detailing the causes of potential violations of the HIPAA Privacy and Security Rules. Notably, in October 2020, the OCR posted four announcements, most with either sub-cases or multi-breaches, of case settlement with potential corrective action plans for violations to the HIPAA Privacy and Security Rules.

5. A risk assessment library

Schmeelk [26] contributed a new open source risk assessment library example to enable researchers, penetration testers, risk assessment managers and institutions to further expand on a consistent risk-assessment findings library with their policies, procedures, organizational controls and legal requirements. As noted in the research bug libraries, dictionaries are being maintained by large organizations but do not include risk-assessment findings, thus complicating risk-management methods. As cited, during experience with internal audits risk assessment, language made analysis next to impossible. For example, modern natural language processing methods would need to take place on penetration tests to evaluate assessment reports among different assessors, each applying different methodologies and terminologies.

5.1 Example risk assessment frameworks

Currently, assessment frameworks are entirely intra-organization. In addition, accessing patient databases is impossible—luckily—in the USA due to HIPAA. That said, NIST has guidance on developing an actual risk-assessment process [14]. However, NIST 800–30, as seen in **Figure 5**, does not actually specify threat source, threat event, actual vulnerabilities, or impact. The actual language used to describe these components is entirely left up to each organization to develop. Even worse, each risk assessor on the team may, in fact, describe these components differently (i.e., use entirely different words). In such cases, making any kind of accurate meta-analysis about the organizational risk is entirely impossible. Therefore, we argue that risk assessment frameworks need a standardized library to describe the identified risk.

5.2 Example findings library

An open-source library example from Schmeelk [26] is seen in **Figure 8** applying an example-consistent risk language. The library needs to be expanded from industry working groups, similarly to MITER's CWE and NIST's BF.

Some important elements for language specification and risk clarification are seen in **Figure 8** [26]; they are the following: vulnerability short descriptive name, vulnerability expanded description, techniques to remediate or mitigate the vulnerability, estimated likelihood factors, estimated impact factors, related organizational policies/standards, related NIST Controls, related HIPAA regulatory requirements, other related legal requirements such as non-disclosure agreements, and estimated breach cost factors for insurance and related required patient identity-theft protection costs/notifications.

These categories listed in the prototype can arguably be expanded or removed. Historically, vulnerability standardization libraries [20–22] are maintained by major organizations (e.g. MITER) and/or government entities (e.g. NIST). Based on healthcare operation needs, we developed the following descriptions of the prototype categories.

Vulnerability	Description	Remediation	likelihood	impact	Policy/Standard	NIST Controls	Related HIPAA	Other-Related-Legal	Budget
System does not employe 2-factor authentication	Two-factor authentication is considered industry best practice: something you know, something you are and something you have	Add two-factor authentication	L - < 3 people M - 1-20 patients or < 100 Employees H - 20+ patients, All Employees or Domain Admins	L - public information M -internal only information H - regulated information	NYS-S14-006 - Authentication Tokens	IA-2 : IDENTIFICATION AND AUTHENTICATION (ORGANIZATIONAL USERS)	164.312 (c) (2)	Non-Disclosure Agreement (NDA)	L - $ ($1K/person) M - $$ ($2K/person) H - $$$ ($3K/person)
System vulnerable to cross site scripting (XSS)	Cross-Site Scripting (XSS) attacks are a type of injection, in which malicious scripts are injected into otherwise benign and trusted websites.	Output encoding and implement content security policy header.	L - < 3 people M - 1-20 patients or < 100 Employees H - 20+ patients, All Employees or Domain Admins	L - public information M -internal only information H - regulated information	NYS-S13-002 - Secure Coding Standard	SI-10 : INFORMATION INPUT VALIDATION			L - $ ($1K/person) M - $$ ($2K/person) H - $$$ ($3K/person)
System vulnerable to improper password complexity.	A password is a string of characters used to verify the identity of a user during the authentication process.	Enforce more complex passwords on the server-side.	L - < 3 people M - 1-20 patients or < 100 Employees H - 20+ patients, All Employees or	L - public information M -internal only information H - regulated information	NYS-S14-006 - Authentication Tokens	IA-5 : AUTHENTICATOR MANAGEMENT	164.312 (c) (2)	Non-Disclosure Agreement (NDA)	L - $ ($1K/person) M - $$ ($2K/person) H - $$$

... Training | Vendor | Application | Policies+Procedures | Physical Security

Figure 8.
Risk assessment library prototype.

5.2.1 Standardizing the actual risk vulnerability and remediation language

The *vulnerability* column summarizes an identified system, data communication, or application weakness. The *vulnerability description* column gives a community-agreed-on weakness description. The *remediation* column briefly explains known techniques to remediate or mitigate the identified vulnerability.

5.2.2 Standardizing the actual risk likelihood and impact language

The *likelihood* column provides standardized language for estimating the probability of the identified vulnerability exploitation given different threats. Currently every organization makes their own likelihood estimates. Organizations on different "sides of the physical street" with identical systems and surrounding mitigating controls, can label the risk likelihood entirely uniquely. The *impact* category approximates potential resulting consequence levels in the event a vulnerability or finding is realized.

5.2.3 Standardizing the actual risk associated with policies and NIST controls

Historically, organizations should develop policies and standards to help the organization frame their own cybersecurity stance. The NIST Cybersecurity Framework [35] (the NIST CSF Tool is seen in **Figure 9**) is one useful guide for developing an organizational cybersecurity posture and policies/standards.

The category in **Figure 8**, risk assessment library for the NIST controls, is relevant to mapping mitigating controls to well-known NIST vendor agnostic controls. NIST regularly updates the NIST SP 800–30 [14] to account for industry trends.

5.2.4 Standardizing the actual risk to HIPAA requirements

As Security and Privacy Rules of HIPAA are major and enforceable regulatory legislation in the United States, the related column in the library connects the findings to potential HIPAA regulations. This mapping informs the risk-management process when required regulatory elements are entirely missing or are in jeopardy.

5.2.5 Standardizing the actual risk to other industry-specific regulations

Other regulations, such as PCI compliance [27], The Sarbanes-Oxley Act (SOX) of 2002 [36], FTC requirements, service-level agreements (SLAs), state data breach laws [29], and research non-disclosure agreements, can also play their roles in risk

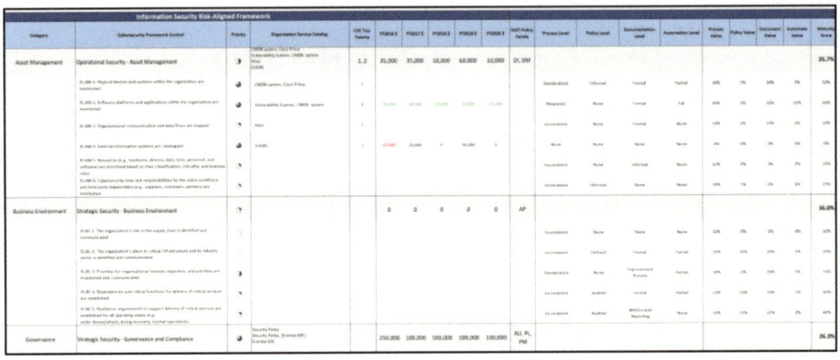

Figure 9.
NIST cybersecurity framework reference tool [35].

management. For example, SOX "is mandatory. ALL organizations, large and small, MUST comply [36]." Organizations allowing customers to pay with credit cards may directly or indirectly be under PCI compliance. The column *other-related-legal* provides benchmark connections to other generic requirements from these related regulations.

5.2.6 Standardizing the actual budget to estimate breach-associated costs

The column on *budget* provides approximate figures for breach and regulation violation ramifications. For example, in 2019, Facebook [37] famously announced a proactive budget appropriation of $3B with futuristic plans to pay off financial penalties related to regulatory breaches. Surprisingly, in some recent healthcare insurance cases, insurance companies have denied financial payouts for healthcare entity victims for malware-related concerns under "Act of Nature" clauses. Such cases of significant financial losses, where healthcare entities are "on their own" for financially responding to the subsequent effects of the malware or breach, can possibly lead to the healthcare entity's going out of business.

5.3 Performance metrics for an assessment risk framework library

There do exist libraries for software development concerns and known vulnerabilities such as the NIST NVD, NIST Bug Framework, and MITER's CWE. They assess their performance. MITER provides an analysis of how the library can be used by stakeholders; however, no formal assessment methodologies exist. Assessing a library framework for performance would be like trying to assess the performance of a spoken language. MITER [38] currently lists the following stakeholders of their weakness enumeration (i.e., framework or library): assessment vendors and customers, software developers and, customers, academic researchers, applied vulnerability researchers, refined vulnerability information (RVI) providers, educators, and specialized communities.

According to Schmeelk [26], the library is currently prototyped as a spreadsheet, similarly to the NIST Cybersecurity Framework Reference Tool spreadsheet representation [35]. Currently, each sheet of the spreadsheet refers to specific domains of findings that can be identified during a risk-assessment process. For example, weakness in the physical, technical, or administrative security requirements would each fall on different spreadsheet pages. In addition, each of these three domains can be further broken into subdomains.

5.4 Benefits from a standardized risk-assessment framework library

Currently organizations are developing their own personal language for describing risk. In fact, many risk assessors within the organizations can actually employ their own personal language. When third-party audits and internal audits transpire, there is no way to assess the risk across the risk-assessment reports. For example, one risk-assessor employee could identify a vulnerability as cross-site scripting; whereas, another may document an XSS vulnerability. If the risk has been described differently by all employees, it becomes impossible to identify how many cross-site scripting vulnerabilities really exist within the organization. Hence, the meta-analysis of risk is entirely flawed. As such, it will be improperly conveyed to insurance companies and third-party auditors. Currently, the only way to develop a unified understanding of the risk is to first develop ontologies of potential words used to describe the risk. Then, perhaps aggregate meta-statistics about the organization can be developed by using natural language processing methods on the written reports. For example, modern natural language processing methods would need to take place on penetration tests to evaluate assessment reports among different assessors, each applying different methodologies and terminologies. As such, most insurance companies and third-party auditors are taking large chances on organizations who really do not understand their own cybersecurity concerns.

5.5 Improvements made by introducing a standardized risk library

Currently, there are no other relevant approaches where the risk language is standardized other than the vulnerability language frameworks of MITER and NIST. This lack of standardized risk language remains a major gap in risk analysis. Schmeelk [26] reports on an analysis for the prototype risk library and connects the library to New York State (NYS) Information Technology Security (ITS) Policies [39]. Standardizing the language used during risk assessments is essential for both internal and external factors. First, if a risk-related case ever goes to court, the phrasing of the risk could play a role in the court verdict. For example, if a business chooses to accept a finding where "unauthorized access" was identified during a risk assessment, the organization may be responsible for accepting the risk. Second, when an organization whose assessments have been written using any plethora of words is trying to collect internal metrics, characterizing the current state of cybersecurity within the organization is nearly impossible. This would be a useful application for Natural Language Processing (NLP), trying to characterize quantitatively exact numbers of password violations, XSS, SQL injection, and other findings. Without standardization, knowing at any time an organizational stance on cybersecurity becomes next to impossible. In addition, remediation efforts and risk mitigation efforts are significantly hindered by text-based risk assessments which do not conform to standards. Lastly, if every organization's employees compose/compile/develop their own libraries, there will be no way to properly coordinate with insurance companies for breach budgeting. Sadly, without any standardization or proper planning, organizations may learn "the hard way" that they are entirely financially responsible for cleaning up a major data breach or ransomware attack.

5.6 Industry concerns addressed by a standardized risk library

The United States and the world are adopting, either explicitly or implicitly, technology-related risk at an unprecedented rate. In addition, regulations are being adopted across the world at an equally unprecedented rate. In fact, each of the 50 United States and "the District of Columbia, Guam, Puerto Rico and the Virgin Islands have enacted legislation requiring private or governmental entities to notify individuals of security breaches of information involving personally identifiable information [29]." Each state law is potentially different from the other state laws, further complicating situations involving out-of-state patients. Most organizations have adopted Integrated Risk Management (IRM) solutions, but many of these solutions require extreme customization from clients. In addition, not everyone in the organization has an overall "view" of the organizational risks. Since Information Systems (IS) trends remain in silos [40], coordinating risk among the different healthcare departments and all the IS sectors is difficult. In addition, entities within an organization that sign off on risk, typically referred to as system owners, may find an imbalance on the risk they must accept on the behalf of the business. Then, as system owners leave or retire from an organization, subsequent new hires may not fully understand the risks inherited with their positions. In fact, new hires in security high-level positions often ask the organization for audits prior to taking, or during the first year of, a new job. That way they can benchmark the inherited risks.

6. Conclusions

As risk management evolves, so do the needs for risk communication and risk articulation. Healthcare entities need to know, in advance, exactly what their insurance covers involving privacy and security risks. Patients need to be aware of identity theft concerns if their personal identifying information (PII) is breached and sold in alternative marketplaces. Technology in the healthcare-related infrastructure is here to stay; ultimately, society will need to standardize how they deal with and respond to privacy and cybersecurity risks. The sooner we adopt a framework of actual privacy and security violations and corrections, the better industry will be able to communicate and mitigate risks—especially in healthcare where human life is at ultimately at risk.

Author details

Suzanna Schmeelk
St. John's University, New York, USA

*Address all correspondence to: schmeels@stjohns.edu

IntechOpen

© 2021 The Author(s). Licensee IntechOpen. This chapter is distributed under the terms of the Creative Commons Attribution License (http://creativecommons.org/licenses/by/3.0), which permits unrestricted use, distribution, and reproduction in any medium, provided the original work is properly cited.

References

[1] Europe Union (2020) The EU General Data Protection Regulation (GDPR). Retrieved from: https://eugdpr.org

[2] Maranto, Lauren (2020) Who Benefits from China's Cybersecurity Laws? Retrieved from: https://www.csis.org/blogs/new-perspectives-asia/who-benefits-chinas-cybersecurity-laws

[3] U.S. Department of Health and Human Services (HHS). (2020). Health Information Privacy, from https://www.hhs.gov/hipaa/index.html

[4] U.S. Department of Health and Human Services (HHS). (2013, July 26). HITECH Act Breach Notification Guidance and Request for Public Comment. Retrieved July 11, 2020, from https://www.hhs.gov/hipaa/for-professionals/security/guidance/HITECH-act-breach-notification-guidance/index.html

[5] Federal Trade Commission (2020) Health Breach Notification Rule. Retrieved from: https://www.ftc.gov/tips-advice/business-center/guidance/health-breach-notification-rule

[6] Schmeelk, S. (2019). Where is the Risk? Analysis of Government Reported Patient Medical Data Breaches. In IEEE/WIC/ACM International Conference on Web Intelligence - Companion Volume (WI '19 Companion). Association for Computing Machinery. New York, NY. doi:https://dl.acm.org/doi/10.1145/3358695.3361754

[7] Schmeelk, S. (2019). Identity Theft: Anatomy of a Data Breach. New York, New York: Parsons - The New School for Design. URL https://parsons.nyc/thesis-2019

[8] M. Catelani, L. Ciani and C. Risaliti, "Risk assessment in the use of medical devices: A proposal to evaluate the impact of the human factor," 2014 IEEE International Symposium on Medical Measurements and Applications (MeMeA), Lisboa, 2014, pp. 1-6.

[9] F. Kammüller, "Combining Secure System Design with Risk Assessment for IoT Healthcare Systems," 2019 IEEE International Conference on Pervasive Computing and Communications Workshops (PerCom Workshops), Kyoto, Japan, 2019, pp. 961-966.

[10] Sonia H. Stephens. 2015. Interactive data visualization for risk assessment: can there be too much user agency?. In Proceedings of the 33rd Annual International Conference on the Design of Communication (SIGDOC '15). ACM, New York, NY, USA, Article 9 , 2 pages. DOI: http://dx.doi.org/10.1145/2775441.2775446

[11] Schmeelk, S., Dragos, D., & DeBello, J. (2021). What Can We Learn about Healthcare IT Risk from HITECH? Risk Lessons Learned from the US HHS OCR Breach Portal. Hawaii International Conference on System Sciences-54 (Under review) (p. 10). Kuai, HI, USA: University of Hawaii at Manoa.

[12] Eddy, M. and Perlroth, N. (2020) Cyber Attack Suspected in German Woman's Death Retrieved from: https://www.nytimes.com/2020/09/18/world/europe/cyber-attack-germany-ransomeware-death.html

[13] U.S. NIST (2020) Cybersecurity Resource Center. Retrieved from: https://csrc.nist.gov/Topics/Security-and-Privacy/risk-management/risk-assessment

[14] U.S. NIST (2012) NIST Special Publication 800-30. Guide for Conducting Risk Assessments. Retrieved from: https://csrc.nist.gov/publications/detail/sp/800-30/rev-1/final

[15] B. Xing, L. Gao, J. Zhang and D. Sun, "Design and Implementation of an XML-Based Penetration Testing System," 2010 International Symposium on Intelligence Information Processing and Trusted Computing, Huanggang, 2010, pp. 224-229.

[16] K. P. Haubris and J. J. Pauli, "Improving the Efficiency and Effectiveness of Penetration Test Automation," 2013 10th International Conference on Information Technology: New Generations, Las Vegas, NV, 2013, pp. 387-391.

[17] H. Radwan and K. Prole, "Code Pulse: Real-time code coverage for penetration testing activities," 2015 IEEE International Symposium on Technologies for Homeland Security (HST), Waltham, MA, 2015, pp. 1-6.

[18] Lei Liu, Jing Xu, Chenkai Guo, Jiehui Kang, Sihan Xu and Biao Zhang, "Exposing SQL Injection Vulnerability through Penetration Test based on Finite State Machine," 2016 2nd IEEE International Conference on Computer and Communications (ICCC), Chengdu, 2016, pp. 1171-1175. doi: 10.1109/CompComm.2016.7924889

[19] A. Blome, M. Ochoa, K. Li, M. Peroli and M. T. Dashti, "VERA: A Flexible Model-Based Vulnerability Testing Tool," 2013 IEEE Sixth International Conference on Software Testing, Verification and Validation, Luxembourg, 2013, pp. 471-478.

[20] MITRE (2020) Common Attack Pattern Enumeration and Classification. Retrieved from https://capec.mitre.org

[21] NIST (2020) National Vulnerability Database. Retrieved from: https://nvd.nist.gov

[22] MITRE (2020) Common Weakness Enumeration. Retrieved from: https://cwe.mitre.org

[23] I. Bojanova, P. E. Black, Y. Yesha and Y. Wu, "The Bugs Framework (BF): A Structured Approach to Express Bugs," 2016 IEEE International Conference on Software Quality, Reliability and Security (QRS), Vienna, 2016, pp. 175-182. doi: 10.1109/QRS.2016.29

[24] NIST (2020) Bug Framework. Retrieved from: https://samate.nist.gov/BF

[25] Lee Epling, Brandon Hinkel and Yi Hu. 2015. Penetration testing in a box. In Proceedings of the 2015 Information Security Curriculum Development Conference (InfoSec '15). ACM, New York, NY, USA, Article 6, 4 pages. DOI: https://doi.org/10.1145/2885990.2885996

[26] Schmeelk, S. (2020) Creating a Standardized Risk Assessment Framework Library for Healthcare Information Technology, HICSS-53: Hawaii International Conference on System Sciences, DOI: 10.24251/HICSS.2020.474

[27] PCI Security Standards Council (2020). Securing the Future of Payments Together. Retrieved from: https://www.pcisecuritystandards.org

[28] New York State (2020) New York State Social Security Number Protection Law. Retrieved from: https://www.albany.edu/ampra/assets/New York Social Security_Number_Protection_Law.pdf

[29] NCSL (2020) Security Breach Notification Laws. Retrieved from: https://www.ncsl.org/research/telecommunications-and-information-technology/security-breach-notification-laws.aspx

[30] U.S. NIST (2002). Risk Management Guide for Information Technology Systems. Retrieved from: https://csrc.nist.gov/publications/detail/sp/800-30/archive/2002-07-01

[31] OWASP (2020) OWASP Testing Guide. Retrieved from: https://owasp.org/www-project-web-security-testing-guide

[32] Santos, O. (2019). Developing cybersecurity programs and policies.

[33] Digital Guardian (2019) What's the Cost of a Data Breach in 2019? Retrieved from: https://digitalguardian.com/blog/whats-cost-data-breach-2019

[34] HHS (2020) HIPAA Enforcement. Retrieved from: https://www.hhs.gov/hipaa/for-professionals/compliance-enforcement/index.html

[35] NIST (2020) NIST Cybersecurity Framework. Retrieved from: https://www.nist.gov/cyberframework

[36] SOX Law (2020) Sarbanes-Oxley Act of 2002 Retrieved from: https://www.soxlaw.com

[37] Jeff Horwitz (2019) Facebook Sets Aside $3 Billion to Cover Expected FTC Fine. Retrieved from: https://www.wsj.com/articles/facebook-sets-aside-3-billion-to-cover-expected-ftc-fine-11556137113

[38] MITRE (2020) CWE Stakeholder Analysis. Retrieved from: https://cwe.mitre.org/community/research/stakeholders.html

[39] New York State (2020) ITS Security Policies. Retrieved from: https://its.ny.gov/eiso/policies/security

[40] Benson, R.J., Ribbers, P.M., and Blitstein, R.B. (2014) Preface and Chapter 1. Trust and Partnership: Strategic IT: Management for Turbulent Times. Wiley. 1118443934

Section 3

Human-Computer Interaction

Chapter 6

A Revolutionary Gaming Style in Motion

Zarif Bin Akhtar

Abstract

From the timeline of the year, 2012 MONECT has been aiming towards the conceptuality for developing the formulation of making a virtual remote controller for a wide range of variety within the context considering various types of devices and peripherals consisting within the prospective realm of virtual controlling. Moving forward, where recently in the timeline for the year of 2017, the including of the functionality of that very same aspect with numerous advancements which was termed and computed as a remote desktop session with gaming control for a wide variety of games which includes games like Racing, Frames Per Seconds (FPS), Role-Playing Game (RPG) along with many more where each type of gaming aspect was equipped with its own perspective type of setup and a familiar type layout for the users who were considered for having different types of controllers for each specific gaming style and associated gameplay render. The project prospect evolved further within the year timeline of 2019–2021 which introduced and revolved around the rapidly deployable features and functionality with integrated advancements in terms of computing and gaming as a whole. Based on that deployment project outcome and developmental scope of the research, the application utilized the full use of the provided onboard sensors to give the user the ultimate experience while performing gameplay (for example, like the Accelerometer sensor, G-Sensor, Gyroscope sensor, Camera sensor etc. with many more). Each of the sensors controlled a different particular aspect of control. For instance, Frames Per Second (FPS) mode triggered and enabled the Gyroscope sensor which would allow the user to aim at their perspective targets for a solid headshot kill. On the other hand, the Race mode used the G-Sensor to enable steering mode of movement in the form of any vehicle. Besides that, the virtual remote sessions brought about the privilege and also gave each user a simultaneous interaction among devices and peripherals with real-time remote access at any given moment in time of usage.

Keywords: Virtual joystick controllers, Real-Time remote sessions, User-associated, remote access, Simultaneous session access, Real-Time interactive gameplay

1. Introduction

Before starting off with the details let us get some terminology of concepts and their usage in terms of computing and processing out of the way with some familiarity. The discussed aspects were altered and customized to provide the final output for the application development.

Firstly, Remote Desktop Connection (RDC) or Remote Desktop Protocol (RDP) is a proprietary protocol which was developed by Microsoft, that provides a

IntechOpen

user with a Graphical User Interphase (GUI) to connect to another computer over a network connection [1]. In order to create and establish that particular connection, both devices required access with one another, for the user who deploys the RDP client software for the purpose that, while on the other hand the other user must run RDP server software. Microsoft concurrently refers to this official RDP client software as Remote Desktop Connection, formerly "Terminal Services Client" [2]. Added that, the protocol which gets established remains a one-way connection, in other words only one host session but no simultaneous interaction among the associated devices [3–22].

But MONECT came up with the conceptuality and the idea for an application which would have a simultaneous session on both hosts or both of the associated devices [23]. Thus, the idea conceptuality brought a fresh new dimension to the context of the research project, and resulted in the PC Remote application [24, 25]. The approach to the solution was that, a device compatible application which would be connected in a network-associated integration both from the user and the device end. So that, no rendering would take place whether if the user happened to be an IOS or an Android or a Windows Phone user. There had been no limitation towards device compatibility. Various features with integrated functionalities had been developed within the application [26, 27]. On the per of that context, how much calibratable the application would be, varied from user to user as each and every user would have a different set of needs from the privileged application and its utility of tools with features. Also, no need requirement for hardware and assembly for any type of parts or components since the application would take advantage of the onboard integrated peripherals of the smart devices. But users had to install the provided driver for the application in order to run the app which was prebuilt inside the application from both the user end and the device perspective (www.monect.com). To run the app, any user can download the main file from Google Play Store (MONECT PC Remote) [28].

For clarity and max performance along with computation, the link for the individual platform was also provided in the website. The configuration layout of the application was built and developed from the Android Version 4.0 which was termed Ice Cream Sandwich for the reason that, the application would have no compatibility issue with almost 98% of apk platforms. Along with that, if the usable devices were equipped with higher versions which would be much better for the prospective users. The installation process was basically download & install, afterwards, it's an integrated configuration with any basic type of Wi-Fi connectivity to connect and run the application. But bear in mind of the fact that, the user needed to be within the same network for the connection establishment. Within this scope of the chapter, the features and functionalities which were deployed from within the application along with the formulation and advancements to the application which will also be described on a further detailed manner.

2. Formulation of the application

Now let us start with the hardware functionality. The Hardware implementation was configured and formulated within the Smartphones themselves. Every smartphone was unique in its own way with both for its features and functionalities, but one aspect that still remained stagnant throughout the course of time was the sensors which were equipped and associated within a particular device.

Since the dawn of smartphones were introduced, our mobility with sensory took flight in the form like camera, proximity, gyroscope, accelerometer, light, ambient aura, motion, pedometer, rotation vector, orientation, touch, magnetometer, thermometer, microphone, fingerprint with many more. But over the passage of time, almost 95% of the smartphones had the majority of all the basic sensors which the application required to collaborate with the devices associated along with it and as for the rest, it was mainly software implementation with various rendering provided from designing, coding, wireframing and terminal commanding sequence of the programming perspective. To minimize the complexity for the functionality and user experience, virtual triggers with touch buttons were placed for the utility feature deployment of the application (**Figure 1**).

Next, the development for the application was built and deployed under three phases where each and every node connection was confirmed with the establishment through the Internet Protocol (IP) associated within the internet network connection. As I am sure, we are all familiar with the terminology of the subnet mask and default gateway for the render of an internet connection provided by the ISP. But please bear in mind, the pathway connection would work only when the user is within the same network [29]. For a better understanding on this matter, let us break down the connection bridge of the communication which mainly takes place and is performed inside an internet connection and how the operation will be executed.

The subnet mask was employed by the TCP/IP protocol to see whether or not a bunch is on the native subnet or in a foreign network. Internet Protocol (IP) Access provides users with an IP address to remote networks. IP Access connects the user to a beacon of victimization which is called an OpenVPN tunnel. Afterwards, the GRE protocol is then configured to bridge this affiliation across the present beacon VPN tunnel established from the node to the beacon, onto the management local area network connected to the node. Whereas when connected, the user will access the IP addresses on the remote management local area network directly, like by the usage of the ping command or by writing them into the browser address bar. To be more specific on the matter, consider this aspect as the back-end computation factor considering our browsers and the establishment of a successful internet connection.

Bluetooth which if utilized properly would also be a source of wireless technology traditional for exchanging information between mounted and mobile devices over short distances, short-wavelength frequency, radio waves inside the economic,

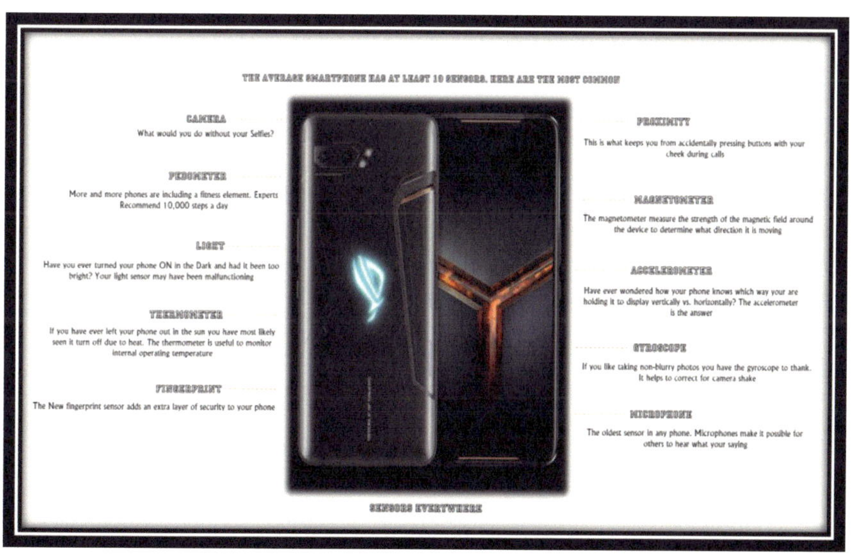

Figure 1.
A graphical view of the hardware components (smartphone).

scientific, and medical radio bands, ranging from 2.400 to 2.485 GHz, and building personal house networks (PANs). IEEE 802.11 is a part of the IEEE 802 set of local area network protocols which specifies the set of the media access management (MAC) and physical layer (PHY) protocols for implementing wireless native house network, wireless local area network (WLAN), the deployment of wireless fidelity (Wi-Fi), laptop computer communication in varied frequencies, also as but not restricted to a tier of four, five and sixty rate frequency bands. These are the protocols which do the square measure.

Typically, square measure utilized in conjunction with the IEEE 802.2, and a square measure designed to interwork seamlessly with the local area network, and square measure fairly and usually accustomed to carry the internet Protocol traffic. The 802.11 family consists of a series of a half-duplex over-the-air modulation techniques that use constant basic protocol. The 802.11 protocol family use carrier-sense multiple access with collision dodging whereby instrumentality listens to a channel for various users (including non 802.11 users) before causing and interfacing with each and every individual packet. A router may need interfaces for numerous styles of physical layer connections, like copper cables, fiber optics, or wireless transmission. It can also support wholesome transmissions which are completely different network-layer transmission standards availing to the current standards provided till now.

Every network interface that is utilized to change the information packets to be forwarded from one gear end to another which is very unique. Routers could, in addition, be conversant in connecting to a pair of or plenty of logical groups of a laptop or computing peripheral devices referred to as subnets, each with a definite network prefix. Once that information is transferred from one device to a unique on an Internet Protocol (IP) network, it's lessened into smaller units referred to as packets. In addition, with that, to the actual info, each packet includes a header that contains the information to help it to induce to its destination, rather like the physical address information realized on a mailed envelope like the traditional methods available. Transmission Management Protocol (TCP) and other rendered protocols which actually are totally different protocols, do their work within the data on the machine, then it's sent to the data process module, where the data packets unit bundled into information science packets and are sent over the network which is inclined with individual users along with their activity and connectivity to the internet.

To succeed in their destination on the opposite facet of the planet, the information packets should meet up with several routers. The work these routers do and performs, is termed routing. Each of the intermediate routers "reads" the destination information processing address of every received packet. Supported to the data, the router sends the packets within the acceptable direction as every router incorporates a routing table wherever data concerning neighboring routers (nodes) is held on. This data includes the value (in terms of network necessities and resources) of forwarding a particular packet within the direction of that neighboring node. Data from those table is employed to choose the foremost economical node to use or the most effective route on that pathway in order to send the information packets. Every packet is sent in a very totally different direction, however, they eventually all get routed to a constant destination machine. As a consequence, to this, using a global positioning system (GPS) navigation it is also possible to track that movement remotely which is also implemented within the current design approach of the application.

Fast forward to today, with the rapid improvement and innovations in technology, most of the communication protocols have given birth to better enhanced and advanced connectivity which are now achievable in terms of mirror cast, NFC, wireless share, screen cast, nearby share plus many more.

Considering for the network perspective among regions with better speed in bandwidths the faster each seeds gets executed.

The author of this chapter has been working with MONECT from the timeline of year 2017 to present and throughout the years there have been major and minor changes deployed within the application. In the year 2019, the author published a research paper [30] with his specific sets of development and integration of functionality and features, including of the virtual remote sessions which the author had developed himself. Afterwards, the application still continues to grow with different aspects of features based on user recommendations and collaborating ideas which has been in effect till now. The custom utility and user interactions will continue to grow in the near future as well (**Figures 2** and **3**).

Figure 2.
The block diagram of the application (segment 1).

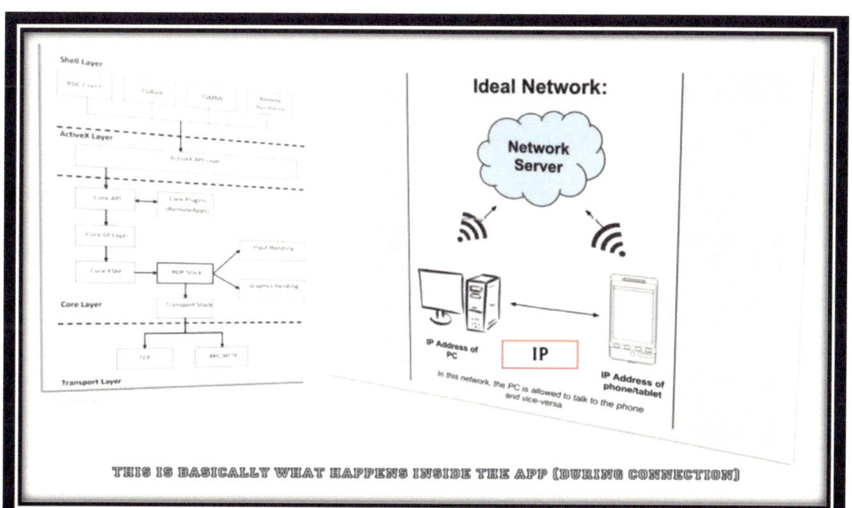

Figure 3.
The block diagram of the application (segment 2).

In order to, use the application, the setup with the configuration was needed to be performed and had to be configured from the user end. At first, from any desired browser the user would type in the link address (www.monect.com) and from inside the website the required steps are given on how to setup the application. The user will select as per their choice from which link, they will forward with the download. For max performance and better enhancement, the software has been upgraded and configured for 64-bit versions to provide the ultimate experience and functionality control for the tools and features equipped inside the application.

Next, in terms of the software integration, the device driver plays a pivotal role. After installation if required, the application, itself will download necessary drivers in the case if any was missing from user machinery (Desktop, Laptop, Notebook). Next, the user needs to provide access and give permission from the firewall in order to allow the connection to be created and established (Pop-ups will be shown when the driver is detected and the connection is established) (**Figures 4–8**).

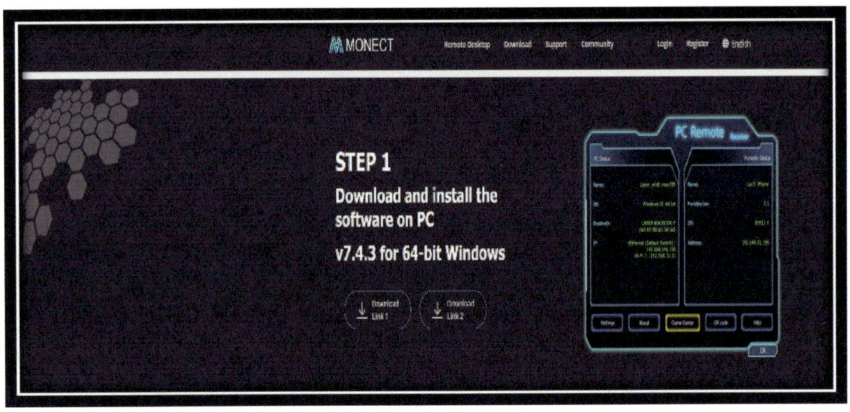

Figure 4.
The website layout with the receiver software distribution.

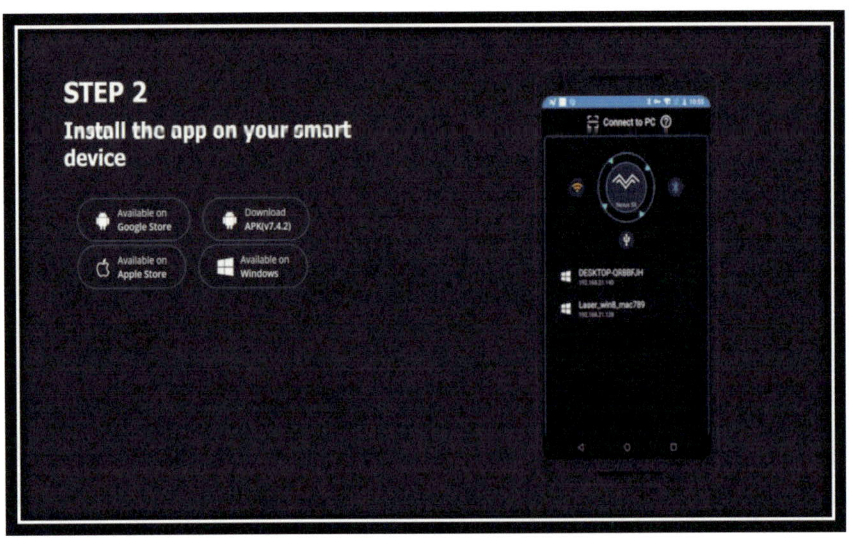

Figure 5.
The software distribution app for the smartphone.

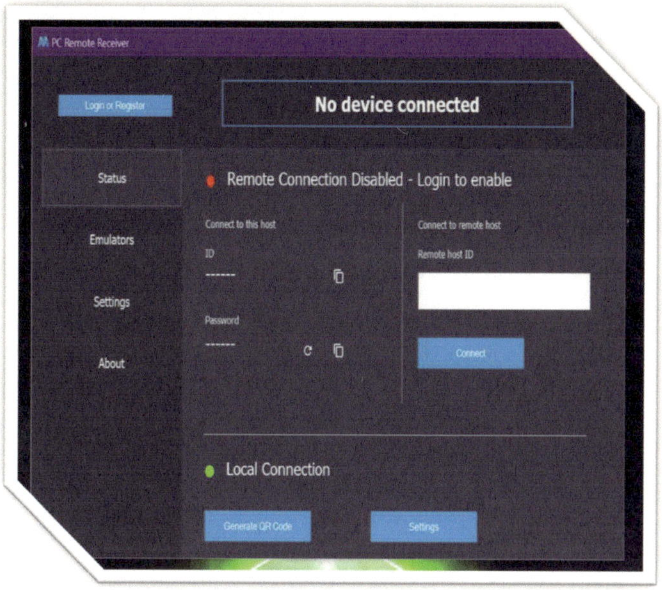

Figure 6.
The software distribution after installation (PC remote receiver).

Figure 7.
The layout design of the app from the smartphone.

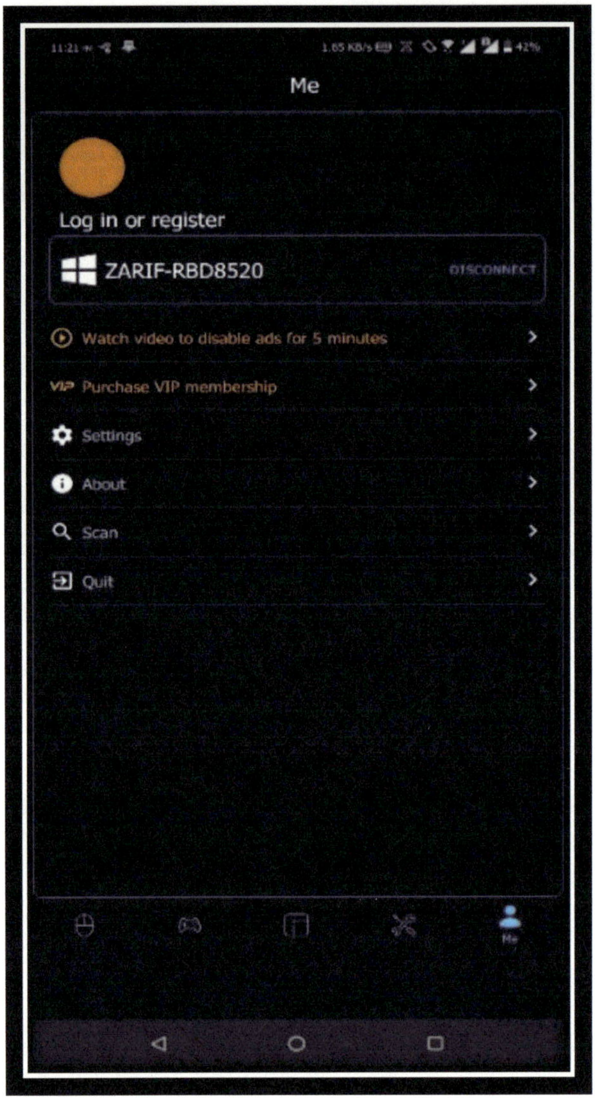

Figure 8.
The layout of the app from an established connection.

3. Virtual gaming layouts

In terms of gaming, a gamepad is an essential aspect concerning performance and accuracy in terms of computation for any rendered gameplay. For a competitive gamer or a noob or just a random player in the realm of shooting, chasing, drifting, controlling, precise allocating of targets, navigation view is of apex value and these are the aspects what determines the outcome of scoring the final win and emerging as a champion for the context on the perspective. Making the apex of head shot kills with the absolute precision and accuracy. All these prospects revolve around the control from the player and his ability of control from his associated device controller. The better the control the higher the probability on the chance of winning. There is a saying that accumulates and prioritize on the matter of selection for a controller that, more frames mean more kills and more frames means victory is at hand with absolute dominance. For competitive gamers it comes to down to the spilt second of a shot which determines the victory outcome for any gameplay.

According to the stats, the gamepad was invented and introduced in the year 1983 which got released later in the year 1985. But in that era of time, it was much complex and very hard to manufacture. After Technological improvements in the recent years, the scale and quality of gamepads has exceeded the gamer expectancy. Still despite all the advancements, it's still a very costly deal when it comes resolving around gaming setup and control efficiency of the associated peripheral devices. The apex root major fact to consider, would be the implementation of the wiring that is associated with its devices.

Next concerning gaming, the setup of gaming peripherals is what alters the course of achievement in terms of performance, efficiency, control and having the optimum machinery. The concerning factor on this issue is the aspect of cost. Cost brings down the scaling factor in terms of machinery and the control for its associative peripherals. Because the better the machinery the higher its cost will be. On the scaling of performance many factors change the perspective of usage and its ability to perform at its level of apex. Graphical computation, frame enhancement, memory mapping, process emulation, terminal sequencing, environment adaption, buffer render varies to a great extent when considering the machinery integration. This limits out the user experience in various states of matters considering for any kind or type of rendered gameplay in real-time interaction.

After the innovation of smartphone concept and its connectivity of control sparked the world, it completely changed the landscape in the realm of gaming and computing to a whole new level. Considering the modern day to day activities our whole assembly of work revolves around smartphones. These smartphone devices have become our daily companions in terms of usage and activity to a great extent. Various technical companies provide us with different sets of smartphones which comes well equipped with many sets of sensors and that is where the application comes to play. The application provides advanced functional utility features which comes well equipped with a variety of virtual joystick controllers/layouts (**Figure 9**). Each of the features provide real-time simultaneous interactive sessions in any given time of usage and activity for any type of gameplay (**Figure 10**).

To make the experience at the level of apex, the user could add and design their personal custom controllers/layouts accordingly due to the fact that, the application was built with the conceptuality of being user-friendly and the scope for its updating was also provided for real-time gameplay sessions (**Figure 11**). Along with the flow of time based on new release of games and their popularity with demand side by side attached with user needs, the layouts will be deployed with updates in each respective time of gameplay and collaboration.

The application had a collaboration with FAMICOM which has been built-in with the app and has an approximate of 31 games included which users can directly open and play (**Figure 12**). And if the user has personal games installed in their PC, then they can directly configure the layout from inside the game settings like an ordinary gamepad or controller. The application will integrate itself automatically. Next, the user just needs to assign the key buttons as per their desire and choice.

What sets this approach above others is the fact that, each prospective had its own set of layouts and if the user desired for any changes or alteration or modification one could make their custom personal layout as well because the user had the option for adding their design layouts. What makes this application unique because due to the fact that, the real-time interaction gameplay with simultaneous interactive sessions for any type of rendered gameplay environment.

For the virtual joystick controllers, its similar to physical gamepads and joysticks when plugged in and configured from user end for each specific key to key or button to button selection. The same functionality and perspective apply to the virtual controllers as well. So, the user can set each key button as per their usage choice and

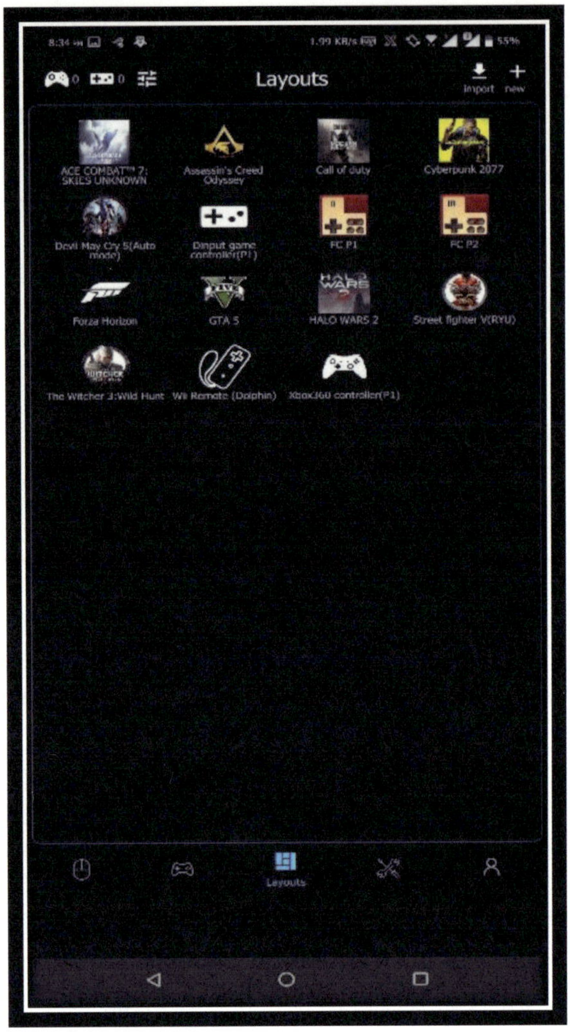

Figure 9.
Virtual gaming layouts for different variety of games.

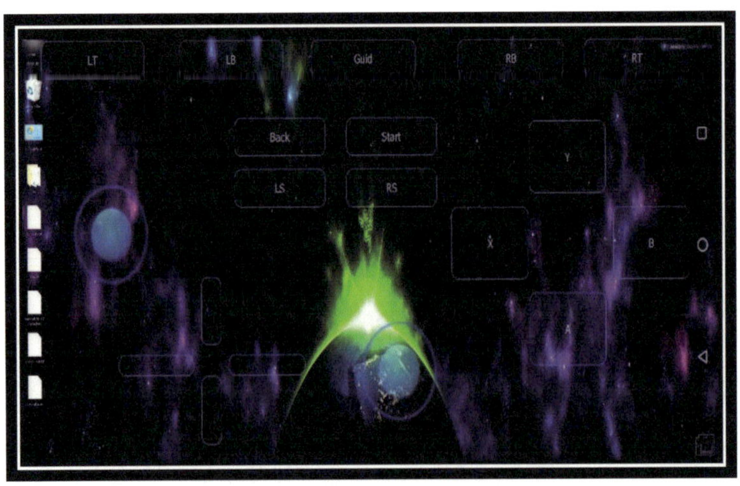

Figure 10.
Virtual gaming layout in a desktop real-time session.

Figure 11.
Real-time gameplay session.

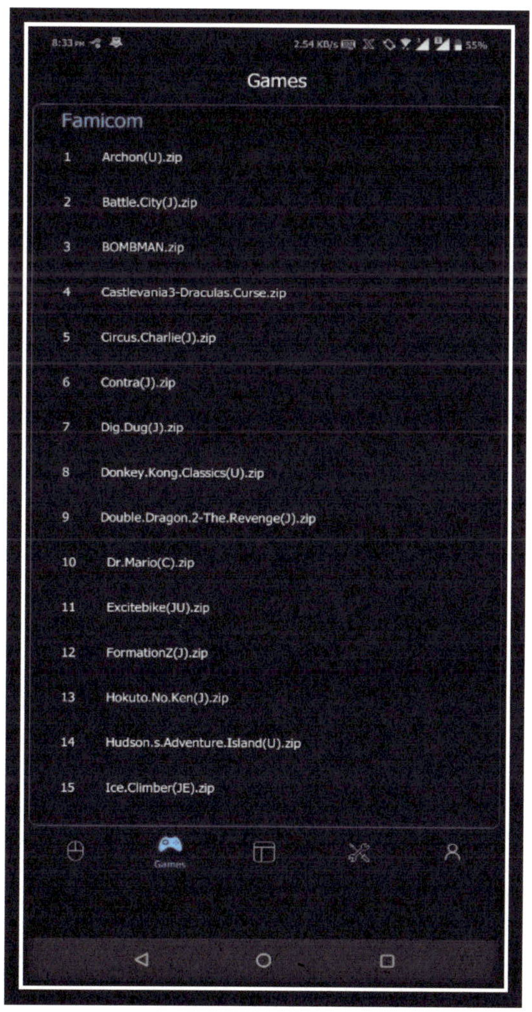

Figure 12.
A collaboration integration from FAMICOM.

then all ready for gameplay. The only difference was that it was virtual & remote and operated in a real-time dynamic session for simultaneous interactions among the associated devices.

4. Remote desktop sessions

Being a windows user and as its usage being revolved around globally, I am hoping that most of us are familiar with Remote Desktop Connections (RDC) since Windows still remains to be the oldest and optimum OS till Now. I know many might have different opinions on the matter which is very much understandable.

As mentioned previously the limiting factors concerning remote desktop connection for one host entry, the application brings a new complete diversity of experience and control concerning remote sessions. The app processes interactive simultaneous graphical interpretation in terms of sessions which are termed as the virtual remote sessions. Each segmented session uses advanced graphical computation protocols which work in both device and from user end for device peripheral associativity [3]. In the case for the Remote Desktop Connection (RDC) the user has access to only one session at a time from a particular host/guest mode while on the other hand, the other mode gets switched to lock screen mode and the connection established works only within a forward path [31]. Which concludes to the matter that, only one host machine processes the interaction. The app development solution overcomes this very issue and at the same time provides simultaneous interactions to users from both ends from a machinery stand point [2]. In order to understand the full scalability of the matter, it would be better to let the users interact and use the application to find it out for themselves.

The designated user also can prioritize control access based on their ability and desire to give access based upon their choices. As it stands out in order to have optimum proficiency in terms of usage and activity the less the hassle the better the experience for the user. Sometimes due to the complexity of certain functionality, many best applications lose their rank on the ladder scale. From that retrospect, the conceptuality for a remote session came about and was developed into a reality. The goal of the feature was to provide an exceptional experience in the realm of remote activity (**Figure 13**).

Apart from the remote desktop session, a variety of utility tools and features were also equipped with the app (**Figure 14**). For a developer, remote access is of immense importance during the layer of design of development for any application or product, or software [32]. As there are many peripherals interlinked with the

Figure 13.
A representation of real-time remote desktop session.

Figure 14.
Associated utility tools from a remote session interaction.

performing of the task for deployment. Even for any normal user having remote access provides ease of work as the interactions are performed remotely. This application gives users access to that very aspect and provides for the integration of microphone and projection from the associated device if required. Many may argue that NFC is a probable solution in this aspect. Yes, that is partially true but for gamers who stream their content or have multiple peripheral usages in terms of computing, this application provides a solution and gives the users a significant amount of control from a remote assembly (**Figure 15**).

For clarity and a better understanding, if a user is working with data or any type of content that is on both devices apart from one another, this app will create a pathway to have precise control on that particular issue (**Figure 16**). Not only that, but users can perform on both devices in real-time interaction from any given session.

In many situations or during research work or performing any particular task most of the time it becomes easier to relocate the information and data based on personal notes and pointers. For problem solutions and brainstorming or generating ideas, wireframing of certain project prospects, the notes play a very significant role on the aspect of the matter.

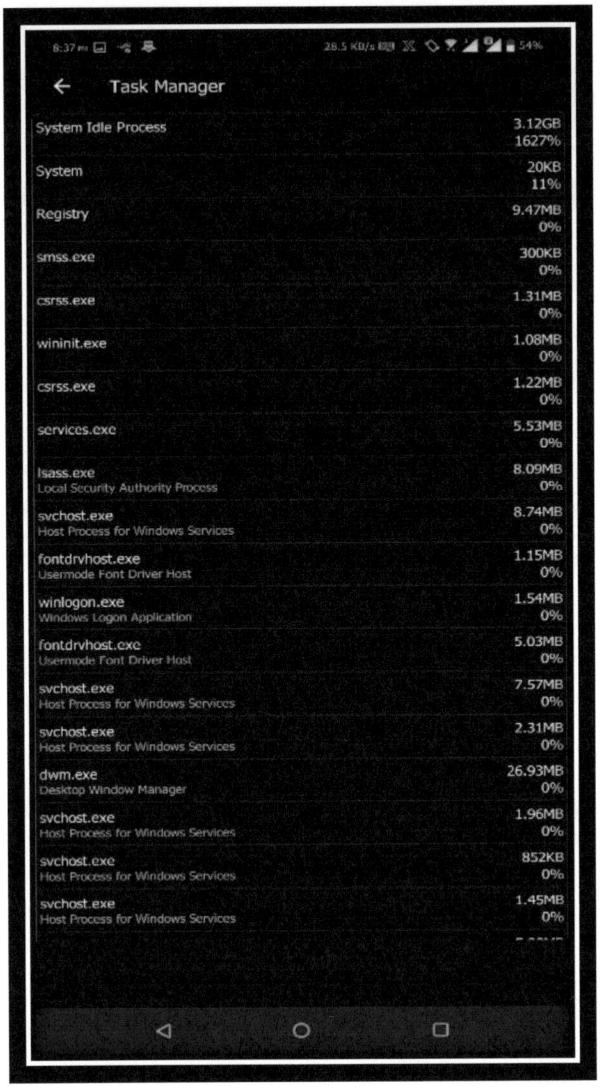

Figure 15.
Real-time interaction of task manager from a remote session.

Keeping that perspective in mind, the application provides a solution on that particular matter through the Blackboard remote session. The user can edit and alter in real-time simultaneous sessions and if required can save the process of execution as a screenshot or photo. Text editing and writing permissions are resourced and allocated from the smartphone interphases and brought to utilization when using the Blackboard functionality. Consider any important document that requires alteration and modification from a remote access assembly from the user end, this functionality will provide a solution in that regard. The Remote Desktop Protocol (RDP) is integrated within the app which the user can use simultaneously both on android devices and the Windows operating systems (OS) and the user would have full access to the windows OS from the associated android device. A taskbar with basic aspects of control was also provided for hovering and zooming around the display considering for detailed fonts or texts. As each display screen size will vary from one smartphone to one another based on users. But if required users can customize the display according to their desired retrospect for clear selection.

Figure 16.
Real-time interaction of desktop PC in a remote session.

5. Additional features and usage

The described features and functionalities were introduced in the year timeline of 2017 and over time were updated within the timeline of 2019–2021. The author had designed and developed these features as a prototype factor and with time each of those functionalities was updated for better performance and usage. The author had published that current research work in 2019 under the IEEE platform [30].

Afterwards, an added feature was introduced and developed by the author for the real-time desktop remote session which is currently in effect on the latest version of the application. The feature gave a full real-time interaction on both devices running at any given working point. Let us simplify the matter with a little detail. For example, let us say the user is currently listening to music from the audio player in his PC, and at any point in time when that user opens the remote desktop session, the concurrent running dynamics will be displayed and processed from the smartphone end with the including of audio in real-time. The same aspect will work for videos as well.

There will be no lag and it will not work like NFC, rather it will work simultaneously for any given time for any state of the process. The user can end the session at any time as per their choice. And if the user opens the session again it will portray the current running dynamics on the PC. Also, the user can control the Desktop PC environment from the smartphone touch sensor. The whole session will give access to the PC end as well. In simple terms, simultaneous real-time interaction on concurrent dynamics from dual devices. Many might be a bit confused on the part of this context. So, the best way to understand from a point of view would be that, use the application and things will become crystal clear. This feature is still found very rarely on today's device peripherals which is the reason why this feature makes the application very unique as many apps have failed to make this functionality available.

Apart from that, virtual remote control for keyboard, PowerPoint representation, multimedia utility, webpage search with Uniform Resource Locator (URL) loader and Operating System (OS) power control like shutdown, restart, lock, sleep, hibernate, sign out and many more along with mouse selection protocol for

Figure 17.
Touchpad control from the smartphone app.

both left and right controls (**Figure 17**). Over the period of years from the user's various requests were made and many design outlets were queried to give a better representation for the control segment and access. After doing various testing and trials on the matter the final design deployments were equipped to the application and was set in motion. It is understandable since in our most daily works the PPT gets used numerous times and especially for working people in the industry it has major usage activity. Based on that prospect of scope and level of interaction in that aspect the provided design feature has been advanced to a certain degree to satisfy the needs. In future this will continue to improve based on need and usage of interactions.

For PowerPoint presentations, this app brings a new dimension of usage in terms of productivity and demonstration of the materials consisting within the slides. One needs to use the utility to fully understand the experience of the functionality and its impact from a remote access perspective. Despite all the functionality considering for the older generation of computers and devices the usage of QR was also integrated (only for older versions). There was a Quick Response code (QR) generator providing users with immediate interaction and connection.

Considering the timeline of usage from the release of the application, the members continue to grow and new users are on the rise even to this day. From the stats of the 2020-year timeline, the app has crossed 5 M+ downloads which is a very big milestone to uphold. From the providing of the free version, there is also a premium (VIP) version for paid users. The features and the functionality of the application were altered and modified based on the user demand and necessity of scope from the future devices. The application will continue to provide future updating for every functionality to give its users the apex of optimum supremacy. Apart from that, the application was user-friendly and ready for use. More new and unique features and functionality would be provided and would be updated which would be available to all the users via the webpage and Google Play Store [33].

6. Conclusions

To put it in a word, the main major difference that came about was the fact that, the users had the scope and opportunity for the operation of the application and if required or needed could alter their customized layouts and directly operate from that assembly. On the context for remote access to the level of degree the application provides is still very rare considering the enormous number of apps available in the global level today. Added that, the computing in terms of gaming and render of performance has brought a whole new dimension to virtual remote access control. Not only for gamers but for any professional or a researcher the app gives a new retrospect to minimize hardware integrity with cost minimization. In today's modern era of computing, a controller for all your device peripherals.

Acknowledgements

The developed & deployed application and research project were built and supervised under the platform and scope provided by Sir Jiang Lei and MONECT PC Remote Team along with the collaboration from the XDA Developers Forum. Under their provided platform and digital layout of the development, the application was formulated and integrated with the features described above and set in motion.

Author details

Zarif Bin Akhtar
Computer Engineering (CoE), Faculty of Engineering, American International University-Bangladesh (AIUB), Dhaka, Bangladesh

*Address all correspondence to: zarifbinakhtarg@gmail.com; zarifbinakhtar@ieee.org

IntechOpen

© 2021 The Author(s). Licensee IntechOpen. This chapter is distributed under the terms of the Creative Commons Attribution License (http://creativecommons.org/licenses/by/3.0), which permits unrestricted use, distribution, and reproduction in any medium, provided the original work is properly cited.

References

[1] Microsoft Corporation. Remote Desktop Protocol. http://msdn.microsoft.com/enus/library/cc240445.aspx

[2] Boldwyn, C., Neumann, S. J., Panjwani, A., & Weiner, M. (2009). What is remote access. Retrieved 16 March 2010, from http://searchmidmarketsecurity.techtarget.com/sDefinition/0,,sid198_gci212887,00.html

[3] Archana Jadhav1, Vipul Oswal2, Sagar Madane3, Harshal Zope4, Vishal Hatmode5, VNC architecture based remote desktop access through android mobile phones, International Journal of Advanced Research in Computer and Communication Engineering Vol. 1, Issue 2, April 2012,98-103

[4] Savill, John (1 October 2008). The Complete Guide to Windows Server 2008. Pearson Education. p. 1752. ISBN 978-0-13-279758-0. Retrieved 1 June 2012. "Windows XP, Windows Server 2003, Windows Vista, and Windows Server 2008 all contain the RDC tool, mstsc.exe [...] MSTSC in the filename mstsc.exe stands for Microsoft Terminal Services Client."

[5] Russel, Charlie; Zacker, Craig (2009). "4: Remote Desktop Services and VDI: Centralizing Desktop and Application Management" (PDF). Introducing Windows Server 2008 R2. Redmond, WA: Microsoft Press. Retrieved 11 January 2014.

[6] Deland-Han. "Understanding Remote Desktop Protocol (RDP) – Windows Server". docs.microsoft.com. Archived from the original on October 17, 2020. Retrieved October 12, 2020.

[7] "Remote Desktop Connection (Terminal Services Client 6.0)". June 8, 2007. Archived from the original on July 17, 2007. Retrieved June 20, 2007. Microsoft KB article 925876, revision 7.0.

[8] "Announcing the availability of Remote Desktop Connection 7.0 for Windows XP SP3, Windows Vista SP1, and Windows Vista SP2". Blogs.msdn.com. Archived from the original on March 8, 2010. Retrieved March 11, 2014.

[9] "Remote Desktop Protocol (RDP) 10 AVC/H.264 improvements in Windows 10 and Windows Server 2016 Technical Preview". Microsoft.com. Archived from the original on August 17, 2016. Retrieved January 12, 2016.

[10] Ragan, Steve (July 19, 2018). "Samsam infected thousands of LabCorp systems via brute force RDP". CSO Online. Archived from the original on December 15, 2018. Retrieved December 15, 2018.

[11] "Securing Remote Desktop (RDP) for System Administrators | Information Security Office". security.berkeley.edu. Archived from the original on October 12, 2020. Retrieved October 12, 2020.

[12] "Windows XP Remote Desktop Connection software [XPSP2 5.1.2600.2180]". Microsoft.com. August 27, 2012. Archived from the original on September 8, 2010. Retrieved March 11, 2014.

[13] "Using Remote Desktop Easy Print in Windows 7 and Windows Server 2008 R2". Blogs.msdn.com. Archived from the original on May 8, 2010. Retrieved March 11, 2014.

[14] "Remote Desktop Connection 7 for Windows 7, Windows XP & Windows Vista". Blogs.msdn.com. Archived from the original on August 27, 2009. Retrieved March 11, 2014.

[15] "[MS-RDPERP]: Remote Desktop Protocol: Remote Programs Virtual

Channel Extension". Msdn.microsoft.com. Archived from the original on April 14, 2012. Retrieved February 13, 2014.

[16] Russinovich, Mark; Solomon, David A.; Ionescu, Alex (2012). Windows Internals (6th ed.). Redmond, WA: Microsoft Press. pp. 20-21. ISBN 978-0-7356-4873-9.

[17] "Windows Remote Desktop Services spotlight". Retrieved 2010-11-18.

[18] "Why doesn't the New Folder command work in the root of a redirected drive resource in a Remote Desktop session?". The Old New Thing. Microsoft. 17 December 2013. Retrieved 18 December 2013.

[19] Berson, Freek (2018-01-12). "The Microsoft Platform: HTML5 client for Microsoft Remote Desktop Services 2016: Remote Desktop Web Client". The Microsoft Platform. Retrieved 2020-05-10.

[20] "Connection Configuration in Terminal Server". Support (5.0 ed.). Microsoft. 22 June 2014.

[21] "Whats new in Terminal Services in Windows Server 2008". Retrieved 2007-07-23.

[22] "Remote Desktop Protocol". Microsoft Developer Network (MSDN). Retrieved 2009-09-10.

[23] MONECT, Copyright © 2018 by Jiang Lei

[24] MONECT PC Remote Copyright © 2018 Monect.com. All rights reserved, Retrieved 27 September 2017, from https://www.monect.com/

[25] XDA Developers Forum © xda-developers. Hosted by leaseweb, Retrieved 30 November 2017, from https://forum.xda-developers.com/

[26] "VirtualBox Manual: 7.1. Remote Display (VRDP Support)". VirtualBox. Archived from the original on November 21, 2019. Retrieved February 27, 2020.

[27] Rouse, Margaret; Madden, Jack. "Desktop virtualization". TechTarget. Retrieved January 3, 2013.

[28] Jiang Lei, "Monect PC Remote", unpublished.

[29] S.J. Yang, J. Nieh, M. Selsky and N. Tiwari, "The Performance of Remote Display Mechanisms for Thin-Client Computing", Proceedings of the 2002 USENIX Annual Technical Conference, June 2002.

[30] Z. B. Akhtar, "Revolutionary Gaming Style in Motion," 2019 IEEE 5th International Conference for Convergence in Technology (I2CT), Bombay, India, 2019, pp. 1-5, DOI: 10.1109/I2CT45611.2019.9033573.

[31] Tang, W., et al.: Hybrid remote display protocol for mobile thin client computing. In: 2012 IEEE International Conference on Computer Science and Automation Engineering (CSAE), vol. 2. IEEE (2012)

[32] VMware, "VMware View 5 with PCoIP" and "VMware Infrastructure Architecture Overview", http://www.vmware.com/files/pdf/view/VMware-View-5-PCoIP-Network-OptimizationGuide.pdf, http://www.vmware.com/pdf/vi_wp.pdf

[33] MONECT PC Remote Copyright © 2021 MONECT (Suzhou) Co., Ltd. All rights reserved, Retrieved 30 May 2021, from https://www.monect.com/

Chapter 7

Improvement of Student Attention Monitoring Supported by Precision Sensing in Learning Management Systems

Andreia Filipa Valada Pereira Artífice, João Sarraipa and Ricardo Jardim-Goncalves

Abstract

A Learning Management Systems (LMS) can benefit from the inclusion Computer-Mediated-Communications (CMC) software for delivering materials. Incorporating CMC tools in virtual classrooms or implementing educational blogs, can be very effective in e-learning platforms. In such student-centered interaction scenarios, it is important to monitor and manage student attention in a precise way to enhance student performance. Sensing with precision through 6G/7G technology allows to include electronic and software devices to produce such monitoring. This chapter contextualizes and describes an abstraction application scenario of sensing and monitoring student attention with high precision in Learning Management System with new communication systems. In that context, technology (e.g. sensors), is used to perform automatic attention monitoring, helping to manage students in e-Learning. Additionally, the document presents a possible scenario which supports intelligent services to the monitoring of student attention during e-learning activities in the context of Smart HEI (Higher Education Institutes).

Keywords: attention monitoring, precision sensing, 6G and 7G networks, Learning Management Systems, Computer-Mediated-Communications

1. Introduction

The Global Higher Education community is nowadays facing new educational challenges due to the Coronavirus pandemic. There is an opportunity for this community to implement a new strategy at the university level [1]. Migrating from traditional or blended learning to a fully virtual and online deliverable strategy is, therefore, crucial to ensure quality education. This transition occurs gradually. Linked to this issue are several questions related to the lack of "home office" infrastructure; skillsets needed for professional design, and online/virtual education options.

Since World Health Organization declared a Coronavirus (COVID-19) pandemic in January 2020, new challenges appeared in the Higher Education ecosystem.

Top ten most affected countries, reported on March 2020, were: China, Italy, the United States, Spain, Germany, Iran, France, South Korea, Switzerland, and the United Kingdom [2]. That context raised the opportunity in on-line and virtual education, to meliorate e-learning, and infrastructures.

The knowledge and skills required can empower workers for future challenges of new jobs that are appearing along with technological advances. Nowadays, it is important to create solutions, simultaneously at operational, services, and technological levels at Higher Education Institutions (HEIs) that can help students develop those competencies.

To date, in e-learning, there is not sufficient research that investigates intelligent technological artifacts designed to enhance student attention through the monitoring process.

Additionally, there is a lack of research in technological integration frameworks that propose design strategies for those artifacts that includes sensitive aspects in education, such as emotions or attention.

E-Learning allows academic institutions to deliver the learning content electronically, both in mobile and online environments. This content might commonly be delivered through Learning Management Systems (LMS). One might say that the tendency of LMS is to become complex when compared with the earlier versions. Nowadays, LMS deals with complex representations of the relationship between resources, teachers, and students, and these systems have become much more customized. These LMS platforms can be implemented by a Service-Oriented Architectures (SOA), a conceptualization that supports the development of web applications. Specifically, in SOA the service provider manages services designed and its implementation. Services are published in the registry, and then will be available for service requests, find the service specifications and the correspondent service provider.

A branch of approaches to e-learning systems focuses on the ability to sense a situation, interface, as well as interact and communicate effectively with the environment. These smart-systems can incorporate sensors and actuators, interacting with other systems, and be incorporated into platforms. It is important to notice that those technologies might be intelligently and methodologically and introduced them into the learning context effectively.

In digital environments, it is important to monitor and manage student emotions and attention. In this work, the term "attention" might be seen as an integration of different aspects or perspectives of attention, aggregating cleverly these aspects. Thus, focused attention sustained attention, selective attention, alternating attention, and divided attention are considered different types of attention and can be monitored depending on the task to be performed. Attention, thus, might be managed in the educational virtual settings, which in this study is done with the support of NeuroIS, a relatively recent branch of information system which allows one to establish a close and fast correspondence between the variables of a problem specification and those of the solution space [3]. Behind that correspondence are the devices that allow one to monitor student attention which is well framed and delineated in the NeuroIS approach. These devices can be used in more complex systems.

Attention-aware systems manage attention using sensory mechanisms, both detecting student focus and making predictions, which allows one to offer customized learning. Several ways have been used for attention detection in the e-learning field, for instance, eye tracking, video, electroencephalogram webcam, electrocardiogram. These mechanisms, for instance, webcam or electroencephalogram, can have an accuracy rate of up to 90%.

The hereby-presented research work encloses the following research question: How to enhance student's attention in an e-learning environment?

Concerning the proposed research question, aforementioned, the authors argue by the hypothesis that if it is possible to sense student's attention based on bio-signals, the e-learning environment can be adapted for each student profile.

The definition of an attention-aware system under the paradigm of IoT could be an available solution.

2. Learning management system

In technological learning, several buzzwords can be found. Most of them are complementary, among them are the terms: e-learning, m-learning, d-learning, and b-learning. Conceptually, e-Learning can is according to Hope et al. "the learning supported by digital electronic tools and media" [4]. Mobile learning (m-learning), is considered a sub-set of e-learning and refers to the portable electronic devices which aim to share content information [5]. Harriman [6] identifies different types of e-learning, among them, are online learning, distance learning, blended learning, and m-learning.

According to Pant & Pant [7], E-learning is "the use of computer network technology through the Internet to deliver the information to individuals". It is a macro-concept that includes both mobile and online environments. At that level, e-Learning is directly related to the concept of Learning Management Systems (LMS), i.e. a web software application used to plan, implement and assess learning processes [8], which technologically supports an educational or learning environment.

Traditional versions of LMS described information learning in a simplified way, we are unable to describe the complex relationship between resources, teachers, students. Recently several more sophisticated LMS architectures have been proposed in literature considering both features of creating and distribution of content; and features that monitor the level of training or training.

Evale [9] proposed architecture to enhance existing LMS through the integration of educational data mining and recommendation systems. In the methodology used to develop the system, the authors considered two different models: the Fayyad knowledge discovery in databases (KDD) process model for data mining; and evolutionary prototyping specifically to develop the system. In a study entitled "A Personalized Learning Recommendation System Architecture for Learning Management", it is proposed an effective personal learning recommendation system to support students via LMS, to enhancing the learning experience. The architecture, based on Moodle LMS, is composed of three main components, specifically: 'learning material data source', 'seeking student information', and 'generation'. The recommendation employs a hybrid filtering technique based on educational metadata and educationally influenced filtering decisions.

In LMS platforms, the material or content can be adapted and change according to the learner's needs, in a personalized way [10]. It allows increasing learner interest, comprehension, and success [11]. Students' performance, has also been recently evaluated automatically in LMS using a learning analytic tool based on some input variables: total login frequency in LMS; time spent in the system; the number of downloads; interactions with peers; the number of performed exercises; and the number of forum posts [12]. The same study, performed with two courses in Moodle, with a total of 171 students, reveals that peer interaction, forum posts, and exercises have a significant impact on student's performance. With increase in popularity of social network tools, such as Twitter similar tools have appeared on LMS.

3. Attention-aware systems

During learning, activity maintains sustained attention important to achieve successful learning. However, it is a challenge to evaluate when students maintain their attention in learning tasks. To maintain student performance in e-learning environments, have been developed attention-aware systems (AAS) with models that consider student's attention states. AAS systems are "capable of adapting to and supporting human attentional processes especially in situations of multi-tasking, frequent interactions with other users, and highly dynamic environments" [13].

According to D'Mello [14], the attention-aware learning technologies, in which one or more types of attention are modeled, are focused on attention. Accordantly, they should not be confused with similar systems that monitor different but related states (e.g. stress, affect, etc.). The automated attention-aware systems in e-learning settings have the advantage of estimate and respond in real-time without interrupting the learner. Typically, attention-aware intelligent systems can both access the current user focus, and make predictions concerning attention shifts. In the attention management field, the goal is on capturing the user's attentional focus, which can be built to offer personalized instruction dynamically supporting learning.

3.1 Traditional sensory-based mechanisms for attention detection in e-learning

This section is dedicated to the most recent sensory-based mechanisms concerning the attention-aware topic in e-learning. In e-learning have been used different sensory-based mechanisms for attention detection. D'Mello [15] refers to emergent technologies, in artificial intelligence in education, those related to eye-tracking and EEG devices. Eye-tracking is probably the most direct method supported by decades of scientific evidence concerning the *eye-mind link* [16] paradigm. While Brain-Computer Interfaces, such as those based on EEG, may complement or replace Eye tracking in the future. According to the same author, other indicators, such as physiology or gestures are undifferentiated signals that encode other information in addition to attention.

Typically, where someone is looking at is strongly associated with what him/she is paying attention to and think about [17]. Eye-tracking is the process of identifying where someone is looking with eye tracker equipment. Current research on multimedia learning has been used eye-tracking technology to study cognitive processes [18]. It allows to measure characteristics of eye movements; usually, there are two main types of measurements: fixations and saccades. The former reflects the attention process, while the latter reflects the change in the focus of visual attention [19]. Eye-tracking is considered one of the most direct and non-invasive ways of study attentional focus.

In a study entitled "Towards Automatic Real-Time Estimation of Observed Learner's Attention using Psychophysiological and Affective Signals: The Touch-Typing Study Case" [20] an experimental study is presented, in which attention is estimated in real-time for the touch-typing task. Results revealed that multiple linear regression models were successful to discriminate between low and high levels of attention. The proposed model is based on real-time sensory data from eye and gaze movement, pupil dilatation, and affective valences of valence and arousal. It is important to notice that this method does not take advantage of saccades and fixations typical used features of eye-tracking.

Electroencephalogram (EEG), already referred to as a "window on the mind" [21] is a physiological measurement used to examine the relationship between mental and bodily processes, in this study related to attention. EEG records the electrical activity of the brain in a non-invasive way at the scalp surface, which is a result of the summed potential currents across membranes of cells. Electrodes placed at the scalp, capture the signal most of the brain regions which are near the surface. Those signals are a) the Event-Related Potentials (ERPs) b) event-related changes in EEG activity in specific frequency bands.

In a study [22], an AAS was developed to identify low and high attention of students based on a genetic algorithm for EEG feature selection, followed by the application of the Support Vector Machines (SVM) classifier. Li et al. proposed an

EEG-based approach for attention recognition using k-Nearest-Neighbor Classifier (KNN) achieving an accuracy of 51.9% and 63.0% for 5-class and 3-class of attention respectively. Despite these classification rates are not high, the authors suggest use EEG along with other techniques such as pressure sensor, camera, eye tracking to have a higher accuracy rate. In a study entitled "Classification of EEG-Based Attention for Brain-Computer Interface" [23] the authors considered 4 levels of attention to be classified into different classes by an Artificial Neural Network (ANN) classifier. The accuracy, in that classification, was on average 63.5%.

Liu et al. [24] proposed a system to detect learning attention using a webcam composed of three layers: 1) image processing for face and eyes detection; 2) eyebrow region detection; 3) classifier. The system, which used SVM for classification achieved an accuracy varying between 89–93%. In a study entitled "Attention Decrease Detection Based on Video Analysis in E-Learning" [25], it is presented a scenario for analyzing individual learning attention level based on the video. It was analyzed using the OpenFace tool [26], specifically: head posture estimation, gaze focus estimation, eye movement estimation (closure and blink); mouth opening and yaw estimation; facial expression recognition. Result achieved an accuracy of 92%. Liang et al. [27] proposed a new technique to recognize human attention state using cardiac pulse from noncontact and automatic and webcam-based measurement. This approach has six different phases: 1) recording images; 2) converting images to RGB (red, green, blue) format; 3) Independent Component Analysis (ICA); 4) calculating human cardiac pulse signals using Fast Fourier Transform Algorithms (FFT); 5) featuring extraction; 6) Classification task with the algorithms: SVM, Naïve Bayes, and Gene expresser programming (GEP) based. Results revealed an accuracy of 81.82%ar in attention detection.

Artifice et al. [28], propose a methodology based on Heart Rate Variability that allows detection attention. The authors argue by hypothesis, that if we define a methodology, the authors can conduct an analysis of attention based on biosignals, then the process to determine better concentration conditions for a person can be facilitated. HRV, i.e., "the amount of heart rate fluctuations between the mean heart rate" [29], have been used to detect ECG data patterns. That variability has been studied in different target populations [30, 31]. In the field of attention, it has been proven a correlation between ECG and electroencephalogram (EEG) devices [32]. The proposed methodology for attention detection is composed of the following phases 1) pre-processing, which is dedicate to noise removal, and detection of correspondent artifacts; 2) feature extraction, refers to the extraction of HRV features, both in frequency and time domain, for further analysis; and 3) data analytics, which aims to inspect data to detect useful information that supports decision-making. A study [33], proposes an attention estimation system with modified smart glasses with inner camera for eye movement detection and, and inertial measurement for head pose position, and machine learning algorithms. Inertial measurement unit allow to acquire three-dimensional orientations, acceleration, and angular velocities. Eye tracking uses Hough transform for central point is the iris, and regions of interest allows to derive the left and right eye corners. Head pose is captured initial data from which are generated. Features, captured from eye images and perceived from IMU data are processed separately for further feature selection procedure through Sequential Floating Forward Selection (SFFS) and computed using Genetic Algorithm (GA) Support Vector Machine (SVM), in which GA optimize parameters of SVM. The system achieves an accuracy of 93.1%.

Sensory-based mechanisms for detection of user's attention in e-learning previously mentioned are synthetized concerning goals, techniques, methods, and algorithms employed, and achieved accuracy and presented in the next table (**Table 1**).

Mechanism	**Studies of user attention detection mechanisms in e-Learning.**			
	Goals	**Techniques, Methods, and Algorithms**	**Accuracy**	**Ref.**
Eye tracking, camera, video	Attention modeling, distinguish between low and high attention levels	1. Multiple linear regression model		[20]
Electroencephalogram (EEG)	Develop a neural attention-aware system (AAS) based on raw EEG signals.	2. Feature extraction 3. Feature selection using genetic algorithm 4. Support Vector Machine (SVM) classifier	90.39%	[22]
	user attention recognition	1. Pre-processing 2. Feature extraction 3. Classification: a. K-Nearest-Neighbor (KNN) b. Naïve Bayes	Higher for KNN: • 51.9% 5-class attention • 63.9% - 3-class attention	[34]
	Attention classification	1. Pre-processing 2. Feature extraction 3. Artificial Neural Network (ANN) Classifier	63.5%	[23]
Webcam	detect learning attention	3-layered system: 1. image processing (face and eyes detection); 2. eyebrow region detection 3. classifier- SVM	89–93%	[24]

DOI: http://dx.doi.org/10.5772/intechopen.98764

Studies of user attention detection mechanisms in e-Learning.

Mechanism	Goals	Techniques, Methods, and Algorithms	Accuracy	Ref.
Webcam	Attention level based on the video.	OpenFace Software, capable of: • head posture estimation – based on Conditional Local Neural Fields (CLFN) • gaze focus estimation – using CLFN. • eye movement estimation (closure and blink) – using CLFN • mouth opening and yaw estimation • facial expression recognition. Uses Conditional Local Neural Fields (CLFN) and Automatic detection of Facial Action Unit based on appearance and geometry features.	92%	[25, 26, 35]
webcam	Attention classification with a new approach Methodology for recovering cardiac pulse rate from video recorders of the human face	1. Camera Recording 2. Convert images to RGB (red, green, blue) format 3. Independent Component Analysis (ICA) 4. Calculate human cardiac pulse signals using Fast Fourier Transform Algorithm (FFT) 5. Feature extraction 6. Classification: a. SVM b. Naïve Bayes c. Gene expresser programming (GEP) based	Higher for SVM: • 81.82%	[27]
Electrocardiogram (ECG)	Methodology for attention detection based on Heart Rate Variability (HRV)	1. ECG recording 2. Preprocessing: Filtering + Artifact detection 3. Feature Extraction: Artifict HRV parameters		[28]

Mechanism	Studies of user attention detection mechanisms in e-Learning.			
	Goals	Techniques, Methods, and Algorithms	Accuracy	Ref.
Glasses (with inner camera for eye movement detection and inertial measurement for head position)	Classification with support vector Machine	1. Smart Glasses a. Eye-movement detection 1. Capturing eye images 2. Capturing eye images 3. Finding iris positions 4. Generated features b. Head pose estimation 1. Perceiving IMU data 2. Generating features 3. Performing normalization b. Features selections (SFFS) c. GA-SVM 2. Attention assessment	91.3%	[33]

Table 1.
Sensory-based mechanisms for detection of user's attention in e-learning.

Considering the current literature in the field, one can say that learner attention in e-learning environments can be estimated based on feature estimation methods acquired from devices as those previously mentioned (e.g. EEG and eye-tracker). Afterward, those features are used in machine learning models of attention enclosed in attention-aware systems.

However, such approaches do not have the appealing characteristics of newer generations of wireless network devices. The inclusion of those devices can disrupt traditional design principles, and thus revolutionize the interaction with the environment in an educational context.

4. Sensing

Internet of Things (IoT) architectures provide means to interconnect people, devices, and to deal with different wireless networks, which regarding its interoperability facilitate the use of smart applications [36]. The progress of mobile wireless communication has allowed to improve sensing systems. One might say that those sensing systems has been continuously adjusted to concepts of speed, technology, frequency, data capacity, framework. A promised field are future generation 6G/7G wireless network regarding its advanced characteristics, expectations. The sixth-generation wireless network enables sensing solutions with "fine range, Doppler and angular resolutions, as well as localizations to cm-level degree of accuracy" [37]. 7G is identical to 6G regarding global coverage, additionally defining satellite functions for mobile communications [38]. On one hand, "new materials, device types, reconfigurable surfaces will allow the network operations to reshape and control the electromagnetic response of the environment". On the other hand, according to the same source, machine learning, and artificial intelligence will allow us to address the major challenges in communication systems. 6G might simultaneously provide ubiquitous communication and provide high accuracy localization and high resolution sensing services. Hight frequency bands allow fine resolution in different dimensions (range, angle, doppler). It allows both active and passive sensing. The former, active sensors emit the sounding waveforms and process echoes concerning the image doppler and angle information. While the latter, transmit natural reflection of surfaces and arrays of pictures, that represents the image. Sensing applications may exploit a vast wider channel with a bandwidth above 100 GHz [39].

Future networks, allows the combination of several materials and technologies in order to create smart innovative contexts. Intelligent Reflective Surface (IRS) [40] technology encloses an array of units, that occur modifications in the incident signal [41]. Those changes may occur in terms of phase, amplitude, frequency, or polarization. In a broad sense, IRS configures the wireless environment to facilitate transmissions between sender and the receiver [42].

Beam scanning technology, it is possible to generate images of the physical spaces, implementing systematic monitoring of the received signals using steering algorithms. Thus, we can create conditions for future "wireless reality sensing" in the university context [43]. Additionally, might be used miniaturized radars for gesture detection, smartphones, monitoring systems with bio-signals. Sensing and location might guide communication sharing mapping information between devices [37].

To date there is a scarcity of studies focused on attention, emersed on those smart environments. Would be important to add new knowledge, studying attention in innovative smart environments created with aforementioned technologies. Specifically, including precision sensing devices and considering the future wireless network generation applied to the study of attention in e-learning. There are promising devices, that regarding their characteristics might be used to study student attention. Traditional devices identified in **Table 1** entitled "Sensory-based mechanisms for detection of user's attention in e-Learning" function as a basis to identify new devices to student attention. Thus, analogous devices might be used in new wireless network generation scenarios. For instance: biosensors, webcam, electroencephalogram, Augmented Reality / Virtual Reality glasses that have recently been used to study attention. Biosensors, highly compact and wearables, have the potential to be used to provide continuous real-time physiological information through contactless measurements. One of the main advantages of such devices is the permeability to adapt to a variety of technological contexts, and its usage within the expansion of wireless communication networks. Next it is described one of such scenarios.

5. Precision sensing attention monitoring of student in e-learning (e-PSAM)

Higher Education Institutes (HEIs) can benefit from using a mix of pedagogical services, including those provided through IoT platforms, such those presented in this chapter.

In that context, it is proposed the "*Precision Sensing Attention Monitoring of Student in e-learning*" (e-PSAM) scenario, which is the students' real-time sensing and monitoring, with emphasis on attention by using technology (sensors, sound, cameras). E-PSAM applies to control engineering devices that are used in order to optimize these processes.

Precision Sensing Attention Monitoring of Student in e-learning (e-PSAM) is the application of Information and Communication Technologies (ICT) in real-time to monitoring student attention. Technology, for instance, sensors (e.g. bio-signal sensors) might be used to continuously monitor the student attention and their behavior during an e-learning task. This allows for helping both students and teachers by supervising and managing their activities. Engineering is used to optimize learning management processes. The focus is on attention monitoring and management. The goal of the e-PSAM scenario is to improve students' attention and performance,

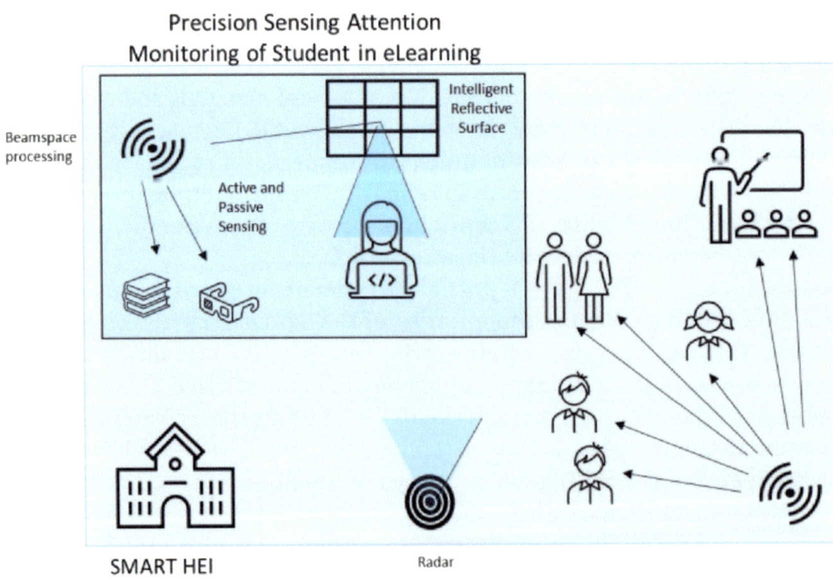

Figure 1.
Precision sensing attention monitoring of student in e-learning in the context of smart HEI.

DOI: http://dx.doi.org/10.5772/intechopen.98764

through monitoring and analysis in the e-learning environment, considering relevant parameters that have an impact on learning and health during the pandemic. e-PSAM management relates these sensing features to provide solutions to monitor, collect and evaluate processes. **Figure 1** illustrates the e-PSAM scenario included in the Smart HEI (the use of smart technology in Higher Education Institutes). Inside the Smart Universities field, which" involves a conceptual modernization of all the educational processes" [44]; it is integrated the proposed approach which encloses future 6G and 7G wireless networks, IoT platforms, and related technologies, as those mentioned in previous section. On the top left it is represented the core of the scenario: a student performing an e-learning task in an smart and monitoring environment which encloses radar and intelligent reflective surfaces. The student might use Augmented Reality / Virtual Reality glasses, and another bio-sensors devices that are instruments used to monitor student attention while performing e-learning activities.

The smart sensing application that supports attention monitoring, at the normal flow, collects and stores variables corresponding to attention measurement. The monitoring processes that will have an impact on student performance are measured electronically. The IoT platform, which supports the system, should be prepared to host the collected data from sensing. Processed information from sensing is sent back to the IoT platform and is made available to all monitoring.

The HEIs are equipped with electronic sensors supported by a new wireless communications provider. It is triggered when the e-PSAM monitoring function is activated. The HEIs stay in monitoring mode until that function is not deactivated, as can be seen in **Figure 2**.

The aforementioned scenario, seen as integrated in a network of HEIs, might be supported by a System-of-Systems (SoS) dedicated to management of HEI data (**Figure 3**). The represented SoS is divided in two main components: one dedicated to the creation environments, and another related to the data analytics which is focused on the management, monitoring, and analytics functionalities.

The system is able to support different data structures, and organized in different schemas, in order to create a knowledge and formalization. Generally speaking, the system supports data volume, velocity and heterogeneity. The implementation would require a cloud platform, envisaging 6G and 7G wireless network and technology.

It would be very useful to study end-to-end performance analysis of the system through simulation in order to derive metrics.

In a broad perspective, the aforementioned "*Precision Sensing Attention Monitoring of Student in eLearning*" scenario might be seen as a possible technological solution to monitor student' attention on a global 6G and 7G wireless network technological environment of HEI Management and Benchmarking trend. Thus,

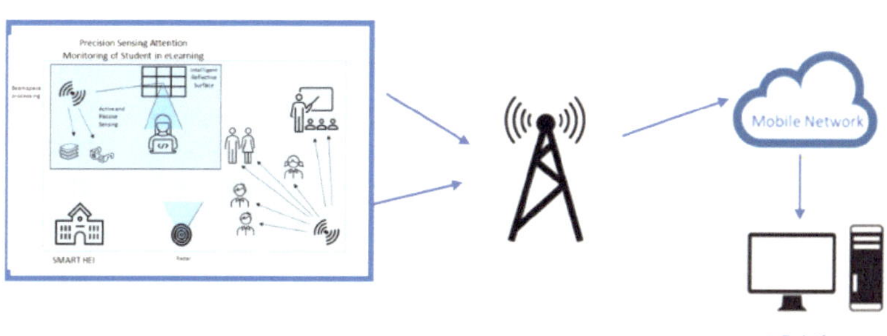

Figure 2.
High-level illustration of IoT data streams and corresponding communication networks.

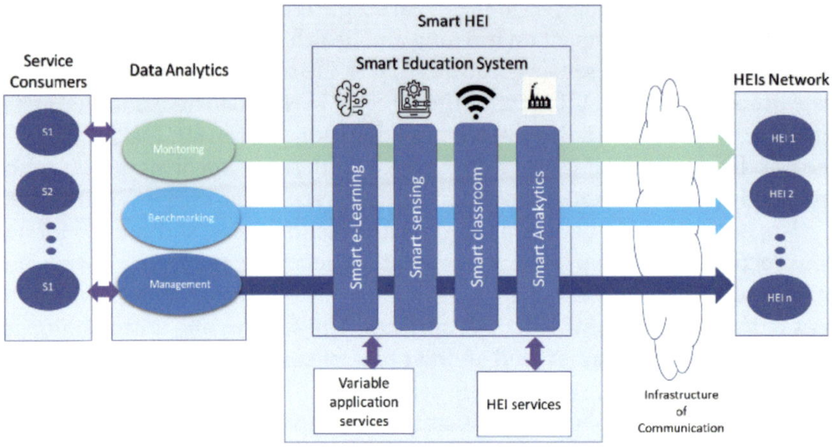

Figure 3.
System-of-systems, IoT based data-centric HEI management.

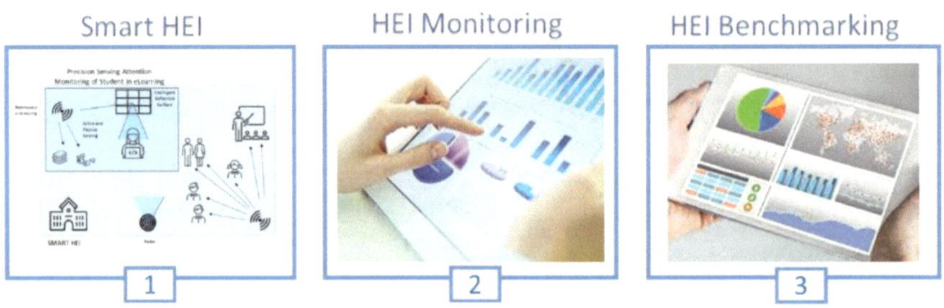

Figure 4.
HEIs management.

contributing to the comparisons of various HEIs processes and performance metrics, giving the possibility to the system to learn and support high-level decisions. In such a case, at the top level of decision, the HEI managers can control the HEIs comparing the results, accepting or not the data analysis results, comparing their results with other HEIs. **Figure 4** illustrates three possible scenarios: "Precision sensing", use case, after equipping the HEIs and learning environment with electronic sensors (step 1), the manager can monitor the HEIs (step 2), through benchmarking with other HEIs (step3).

The solution might benefit different stakeholders in the chain: universities, students, centers of excellence, teachers; and IoT Devices manufacturers, communication network suppliers, and IoT platforms providers. HEIs managers profit from data analytics management services since they might take decisions based on HEIs they are responsible for and benchmarking. IoT platform with acts at the level of platform collecting data from the university. Additionally, it is appropriated to monitor health conditions of the HEI population through sense which seems to be crucial in the pandemic period.

6. Conclusions and future work

Taking what was said into consideration, in the Smart Universities context, endowed with high technology, such as next generation wireless networks and connected materials, is presented e-PSAM scenario, i.e. "Precision Sensing Attention Monitoring of Student in eLearning". Smart sensing monitoring, with focus on student attention might be monitored and managed in e-Learning context with devices, such as electrocardiogram, smart glasses, electroencephalogram.

The ideal technological environment to accomplish such achievements might be supported by IoT platforms with special emphasis on data centric management. Presented ideas will start to be experimented, implemented, tested, and validated, in the context of SHYFTE project – Build skills 4.0 through University and Enterprise Collaboration. Additionally, the project aims to implement a Center of Excellence network; bringing together academy and industry in a symbiotic relation, in order to manage productivity and human labour.

Acknowledgements

The SHYFTEproject referred by "598649-EPP-1-2018-1-FR-EPPKA2-CBHE-JP" has been funded with support fromthe EuropeanCommission. This publication reflects the views onlyof the authors, and the Commission cannot be held responsibleor any use which may be made of the information contained therein.

Author details

Andreia Filipa Valada Pereira Artífice*, João Sarraipa and Ricardo Jardim-Goncalves
NOVA School of Science and Technology, Portugal

*Address all correspondence to: a.artifice@campus.fct.unl.pt

IntechOpen

© 2021 The Author(s). Licensee IntechOpen. This chapter is distributed under the terms of the Creative Commons Attribution License (http://creativecommons.org/licenses/by/3.0), which permits unrestricted use, distribution, and reproduction in any medium, provided the original work is properly cited.

References

[1] M. A. Flores and A. Swennen, "The COVID-19 pandemic and its effects on teacher education," Eur. J. Teach. Educ., vol. 43, no. 4, pp. 453-456, 2020, doi: 10.1080/02619768.2020.1824253.

[2] W. H. Organization., "WHO Director-General's opening remarks at the media briefing on COVID-19," 2020. https://www.who.int/dg/speeches/detail/ who-director-general-s-opening-remarks-at-the-mediabriefing-on-COVID-19---11-march-2020.

[3] R. Riedl, F. D. Davis, and A. R. Dennis, "On the Foundations of NeuroIS : Reflections on the Gmunden Retreat 2009 On the Foundations of NeuroIS : Reflections on the Gmunden Retreat," vol. 27, 2010, doi: 10.17705/1CAIS.02715.

[4] H. U. Hoppe, R. Joiner, M. Milrad, and M. Sharples, "Technologies in Education," pp. 255-259, 2003.

[5] W. Miller, "iTeaching and Learning Tablets," Libr. Technol. Rep., vol. 48, no. 8, pp. 54-60, 2012.

[6] S. Kumar Basak, M. Wotto, and P. Bélanger, "E-learning, M-learning and D-learning: Conceptual definition and comparative analysis," E-Learning Digit. Media, vol. 15, no. 4, pp. 191-216, 2018, doi: 10.1177/2042753018785180.

[7] T. Pant and S. Pant, "The Technology Shift for MOOC-Based Libraries: The Need of Libraries for MOOCs," in *Handbook of Research on Emerging Trends and Technologies in Library and Information Science*, 2020, pp. 109-118.

[8] "learning management systems (LMS)." https://searchcio.techtarget.com/definition/learning-management-system (accessed May 13, 2019).

[9] D. S. Evale, "L EARNING M ANAGEMENT S YSTEM WITH P REDICTION M ODEL AND C OURSE - CONTENT R ECOMMENDATION M ODULE," vol. 16, pp. 437-457, 2017.

[10] S. Thalmann, "Adaptation criteria for the personalised delivery of learning materials : A multi-stage empirical investigation," vol. 30, no. 1, pp. 45-60, 2014.

[11] E. Triantafillou, A. Pomportsis, S. Demetriadis, and E. Georgiadou, "The value of adaptivity based on cognitive style: an empirical study," vol. 35, no. 1, pp. 95-106, 2004.

[12] J. S. Mtebe, "U SING L EARNING A NALYTICS TO P REDICT S TUDENTS ' P ERFORMANCE IN M OODLE L EARNING M ANAGEMENT S YSTEM :," pp. 1-13, 2017, doi: 10.1002/j.1681-4835.2017.tb00577.x.

[13] C. Roda and J. Thomas, "Attention Aware Systems," *Encyclopedia of Human Computer Interaction*. IGI Global, pp. 38-44, 2006.

[14] S. K. D'Mello, "Gaze-Based Attention-Aware Cyberlearning Technologies," in *Mind, Brain and Technology: Learning in the Age of Emerging Technologies*, 2018.

[15] A. I. Educ, I. A. Intelligence, and E. Society, "Giving Eyesight to the Blind: Towards Attention-Aware AIED," pp. 645-659, 2016, doi: 10.1007/s40593-016-0104-1.

[16] M. A. Just and P. A. Carpenter, "A theory of reading: From eye fixations to comprehension," Psychol. Rev., vol. 87, pp. 329-354, 1980.

[17] A. Bojko, *EYE TRACKING THE USER EXPERIENCE a practical guide to research*. Louis Rosenfeld, 2013.

[18] E. Alemdag and K. Cagiltay, "A systematic review of eye tracking research on multimedia learning," *Comput. Educ.*, no. 125, pp. 413-428, 2018, doi: 10.1016/j.compedu. 2018.06.023.

[19] T. van Gog and H. Jarodzka, "Eye Tracking as a Tool to Study and Enhance Cognitive and Metacognitive Processes in Computer-Based Learning Environments," in *International handbook of metacognition and learning technologies*, New York, NY.: Springer, 2013, pp. 143-156.

[20] M. Meža, J. Košir, G. Strle, A. Košir, and S. Member, "Towards Automatic Real-Time Estimation of Observed Learner's Attention Using Psychophysiological and Affective Signals : The Touch-Typing Study Case," vol. 5, pp. 27043-27060, 2017.

[21] P. L. Nunez and R. Srinivasan, "A theoretical basis for standing and traveling brain waves measured with humanEEG with implications for an integrated consciousness," Clin. Neurophysiol., vol. 117, no. 11, pp. 2424-2435, 2006.

[22] S. M. Yang, C. M. Chen, and C. M. Yu, "Assessing the Attention Levels of Students by Using a Novel Attention Aware System based on Brainwave Signals," in *IIAI 4th International Congress on Advanced Applied Informatics*, 2015, pp. 379-384, doi: 10.1109/IIAI-AAI.2015.224.

[23] M. Mohammadpour, "Classification of EEG-Based Attention for Brain Computer Interface," pp. 34-37, 2017.

[24] C. Liu, P. Chang, and C. Huang, "Using Eye-tracking and Support Vector Machine to Measure Learning Attention in eLearning," vol. 311, pp. 9-14, 2013, doi: 10.4028/www.scientific.net/ AMM.311.9.

[25] L. Wang, "Attention Decrease Detection Based on Video Analysis in E-Learning," pp. 166-179, 2018.

[26] T. Baltrušaitis, P. Robinson, and L. P. Morency, "OpenFace: an open source facial behavior analysis toolkit," 2016.

[27] D. Jiang, B. Hu, Y. Chen, Y. Xue, W. Li, and Z. Liang, "Recognizing the human attention state using cardiac pulse from the noncontact and automatic-based measurements," Soft Comput., vol. 22, pp. 3937-3949, 2017, doi: 10.1007/s00500-017-2604-9.

[28] A. Artifice, J. Sarraipa, and R. Jardim-Goncalves, "Methodology for Attention Detection based on Heart Rate Variability," 2018.

[29] C. M. van Ravenswaaij-Arts, L. A. Kollee, J. C. Hopman, G. B. Stoelinga, and H. B. van Geijn, "Heart Rate Variability," *European Heart Journal*, vol. 17, no. 5. Annals of internal medicine, pp. 354-381, 1993, doi: 10.1161/01. CIR.93.5.1043.

[30] J. E. Richards and B. J. Casey, "Heart Rate Variability During Attention Phases in Young Infants," Psychophysiology, vol. 28, no. 1, pp. 43-53, 1991, doi: 10.1111/j.1469-8986.1991.tb03385.x.

[31] L. Col, K. Tripathi, C. Mukundan, and L. T. Mathew, "Attentional modulation of heart rate variability (HRV) during execution of PC based cognitive tasks," *Ind J Aerosp. Med IJASM*, vol. 47, no. 471, pp. 1-10, 2003, Accessed: Dec. 05, 2017. [Online]. Available: http://medind.nic.in/iab/t03/ i1/iabt03i1p1.pdf.

[32] A. Belle, R. H. Hargraves, and K. Najarian, "An automated optimal engagement and attention detection system using electrocardiogram," Comput. Math. Methods Med., vol. 2012, 2012, doi: 10.1155/2012/528781.

[33] O. T. C. Chen, P. C. Chen, and Y. T. Tsai, "Attention estimation system via smart glasses," *2017 IEEE Conf. Comput. Intell. Bioinforma. Comput. Biol. CIBCB 2017*, 2017, doi: 10.1109/CIBCB.2017.8058565.

[34] X. Li, B. Hu, Q. Dong, W. Campbell, P. Moore, and H. Peng, "EEG-based Attention Recognition," in *6th International Conference on Pervasive Computing and Applications*, 2011, no. Ci, pp. 196-201.

[35] T. Baltrušaitis, M. Mahmoud, and P. Robinson, "Cross-dataset learning and person-specific normalisation for automatic Action Unit detection," in 11th IEEE International Conference and Workshops on Automatic Face and Gesture Recognition (FG), 2015, pp. 1-6.

[36] R. C. Clark and R. E. Mayer., *E-learning and the science of instruction: Proven guidelines for consumers and designers of multimedia learning*. John Wiley & Sons, 2016.

[37] A. Bourdoux *et al.*, "6G White Paper on Localization and Sensing," *arXiv*, pp. 1-38, 2020.

[38] R. P. Tidke, P. S. Uttarwar, D. S. Dandwate, and U. J. Tupe, "A Literature Review On : Wireless Technologies From 0G to 7G," vol. 4, no. 6, pp. 59-64, 2020.

[39] T. S. Rappaport and Y. Xing, "Wireless Communications and Applications Above 100 GHz : Opportunities and Challenges for 6G and Beyond," pp. 78729-78757, 2020.

[40] C. Huang, C., Zappone, A., Alexandropoulos, G. C., Debbah, M., & Yuen, "Reconfigurable intelligent surfaces for energy efficiency in wireless communication.," in *IEEE Transactions on Wireless Communications*, 2019, pp. 4157-4170.

[41] & Z. Basar, E., Di Renzo, M., De Rosny, J., Debbah, M., Alouini, M. S., "Wireless communications through reconfigurable intelligent surfaces," IEEE access, vol. 7. 2019.

[42] Wu and R. Zhang, "owards smart and reconfigurable environment:Intelligent reflecting surface aided wireless network," IEEE Communi-cations Magazine, 2019.

[43] O. Kanhere, S. Ju, Y. Xing, and T. S. Rappaport, "Map-assisted millimeter wave localization for accurate position location," *2019 IEEE Glob. Commun. Conf. GLOBECOM 2019 - Proc.*, pp. 2-7, 2019, doi: 10.1109/GLOBECOM38437.2019.9013365.

[44] L. Vinet and A. Zhedanov, "Development of strategyfor smart University," J. Phys. A Math. Theor., vol. 44, no. 8, pp. 1689-1699, 2011, doi: 10.1088/1751-8113/44/8/085201.

Chapter 8

Integration of ICT into Education: Lessons Learnt at the State University of Zanzibar and the Midlands State University in Zimbabwe

Shephard Pondiwa, Umayra El Nabahany and Margaret Phiri

Abstract

The provision of education using ICT has been adopted by many institutions in Africa. The use of ICT is critical in knowledge-based societies such as those in Zanzibar and Zimbabwe. This study looks at how the Midlands State University (MSU) and State University of Zanzibar (SUZA) have adopted the use of ICT in many ways. ICTs do not work for everyone in the same way. It has become inevitable, in the current digital era for educators to integrate ICT in their teaching and gradually replace traditional teaching methods with modern ones which are ICT led. The main objective of this study is to find out challenges and opportunities of using ICT in education.

Keywords: ICT, Integration, Midlands State University, State University of Zanzibar, Education

1. Introduction

There has been an increase in the use of educational technologies in higher education over the last decades [1]. The adoption and use of ICT has transformed education in a number of ways over the years. It has changed the way people think, work and live [2]. While teachers are sometimes seen as key players in the using ICT [3], students have also proved to be relevant and important stakeholders as their needs spur teachers and institutional administrators to be innovative. While it may be correct to say, "The adoption of educational technology in teaching depends on how well a teacher accepts it" [4] we argue that the success of the integration of ICT in education also depends on how much exposure and interest the learners have in ICT. This study focused on SUZA and MSU. While all other universities in the both Zanzibar and Zimbabwe have adopted the use of ICT in one way or the other, these two were chosen on the basis that they have the largest number of both lecturers and students and the study sought to investigate the impact of the adoption of ICT in education. The two institutions are state-funded and such the study examined the contribution of the state in ICT integration initiatives. The integration of ICT into education involves the use of computer-based communication into daily classroom activities. It also means technology-based teaching and learning which contributes a lot in the pedagogical aspects where ICT application leads to effective learning.

Globalization has provided challenges that require educational institutions to embrace technology in learning and teaching. This is important because technology has become the knowledge transfer highway in most countries [3]. Conventional learning set-ups of the brick and mortar classroom have been overtaken by digital environments and the face-to-face mode of tuition delivery is fast being replaced by online articulated learning and knowledge delivery methods. Education experts argue that bringing ICTs into the learning environment will create opportunities for broader education initiatives that will bring pupils into the information era [5].

2. Adoption of the use of ICT at SUZA

The State University of Zanzibar started to integrate the use of ICT in its teaching and learning in the beginning of 2006. It started with the introduction of a simple E-learning platform (ZALONGWA) whereby the lecturers shared the lecture notes and assessments only. The platform was very limited in terms of students and teachers' interactions for example, students were not able to post, comment or delete anything. Things started to change when the Danish International Development Agency (DANIDA) supported project of Building Stronger Universities (BSU) was initiated in 2011.

The project funded the introduction, modification and implementation of the better e-learning platform. Moodle at SUZA from 2012 to 2019. This platform is more useful and allows online interaction among its users. A number of activities have been taking place at SUZA to ensure that ICT is used effectively in teaching and learning. These activities include (1) capacity development (including educational video production, OER integration and production), (2) mapping of students and lecturers' use of ICT and MOODLE and (3) development of guidelines and procedures [1].

Additionally, the university has been very supportive in making sure the infrastructures are there to support the integration of ICT in teaching and learning. Computer labs with access to internet, introduction of a Center for Digital Learning which records and airs teaching programmes to help the students across Zanzibar and production of a first ever Kiswahili Massive Open Online Course (MOOC) [6].

3. Adoption of the use of ICT at MSU

The use of ICT in learning institutions such as the Midlands State University in Zimbabwe must be understood in the context of the Millennium Development Goals that were set by the United Nations in the year 2000.These goals highlighted on the importance of computer technology in the global development agenda. The Zimbabwean government in its quest to achieve the millennium development goals developed a national Information and Communication Technologies (ICT) policy in the year 2005.

The ICT policy was also influenced by a host of other policies such as the Nziramasanga Education Commission Report of the year 1999, the national science and technology policy of 2002 and the vision 2020 policy. In particular, the Nziramasanga Commission recommended in support of the use and application of computers for teaching and learning in educational institutions. The National ICT policy that was adopted in 2005 makes significant references to the promotion of ICTs in education including their pedagogical use in educational institutions [7].

The integration of ICTs in the Zimbabwe teacher education curriculum was achieved through the CITEP (College information enhancement programme). This was a programme that targeted teacher training and polytechnic colleges. This programme did not initially involve universities. Universities and other educational institutions gradually embraced ICT in one way or another. It must be noted that the adoption of ICT at teachers' colleges in a way paved the way for universities to implement the use of ICT because some students came to university when they had had some basic knowledge of the use of ICT while in high school or at other colleges. Government also supported the Integration through providing funding and seeking donations for computer hardware and other related gadgets that are used in ICT. The Integration of ICT into teaching at MSU like at any other government educational institution is therefore, a development that was supported by both government and the university management.

4. Theoretical background

The study is informed by the Technology Acceptance Model (TAM). This is a model based on the understanding that technologies need to be accepted by teachers or students in the first place before considering training them to use technologies for various purposes. In this paper we emphasize that there is a relationship between acceptance and adoption. TAM postulates that the behavioral intention (BI) to use a technology depends on the potential user's attitude towards the technology, which in turns depends on the perceived usefulness and perceived ease of use [8, 9].

This model is relevant in this study in that the use of ICT at both MSU and SUZA was motivated by global developments which necessitated its adoption in the two institutions. Technological advancements on the job market as well as the adoption of ICT by other stakeholders that the two institutions deal with also helped to change the attitude towards ICT usage by the two institutions.

5. Methodology

The study employed a case study approach to study the integration of ICT in education at Midlands State University and the State University of Zanzibar. A case study is an empirical inquiry that investigates a contemporary phenomenon in depth and with-in its real-life context, especially when the boundaries between phenomenon and con-text are not clearly evident [9:18]. The study used a total of 100 University workers and 150 students from the two institutions. 60 of the workers were from MSU and 40 from SUZA. Of the 150 students, 100 were form MSU whilst 50 were from SUZA. The study purposively selected the Directors of ICT of the two institutions and the rest of the respondents were randomly selected. This comparative analysis of the two institutions helped to make a closer look at the differences and similarities in the adoption and use of ICT in the two institutions.

6. Data collection instruments

Two questionnaires were developed and used. One was used to collect data from lecturers from the two institutions while another was used to collect data from students. Interviews were also conducted with randomly selected lecturers and students, as well as the Directors of ICT.

7. Results

Results from the study indicated that there has been the integration of ICT in education at both the SUZA and MSU and this has greatly changed the way teaching and learning take place at the two institutions. The integration of ICT in education has been influenced by the fact that the major stakeholders of the two institutions which are government, lecturers and students have embraced the use of ICT this is in line with the technology acceptance model where adoption of technology largely depends on it been accepted by the users. This section presents results from the study and these will be presented separately starting with the findings from the Midlands State University.

7.1 MSU

7.1.1 ICT in lectures and learning centers

Since inception in 1999, MSU has made strides in promoting the use of ICT in education. There is a compulsory module (course) that is done by all first-year students who enroll at the institution. The module is called Introduction to computer applications. This is meant to equip all the learners with basic skills of using ICT. Most of the students who enroll at the MSU come from high schools which do not have ICT infra-structure and as such they need such a module. As a way of encouraging the use of ICT in education, most lecturers have encouraged students to submit their assignments online. This has gone a long way in promoting the appreciation and use of ICT. By integrating ICT as a learning resource during regular classes, lecturers expose students to innovative ways of learning [10]. This was a departure from the traditional way of hand written assignments which would be collected physically by a class representative and dropped in pigeon holes of lecturers.

The Midlands State University had an ODL programme in which teachers were enrolled for Bachelor of Science degree in computer science. The programme was sponsored by UNICEF and it aimed to equip teachers with ICT skills.

MSU has 9 faculties and each of these faculties has a dedicated computer lab and this enables students to access information on the internet. This means that every student at MSU can access information communication technology while they are on campus. Apart from the faculty labs, the university has a computer center in the city center where every student and members of staff can access without having to travel to the main campus.

7.1.2 E-learning services

According to [11] the internet has become one of the vital ways to make available resources for research and learning for both teachers and students to share and acquire information. Since 2005 every student at MSU has had an e-learning account. It enables students and lecturers to interact using ICT. Lecturers and administrators post teaching materials to their students via the e-learning platform. Examination results are also posted on the e-learning platform. This is a change from the traditional approach where results were displayed on notice boards.

7.1.3 Social media

One way through which MSU has integrated ICT in education is through the use of social media. [12] state that web 2.0 such as social media, collaborative tools Wikis and others are among the emerging technologies that are used in higher learning institutions in developed and developing countries. The study found out that some lecturers have opened up social media platforms that they use to post learning material. Even though there was no official social media policy at MSU until January 2021, students, lecturers and University administrators have gone on to use social media platforms such as WhatsApp, Twitter and Face book to share information and knowledge. Learning and teaching has taken place on social media platforms [13].

7.1.4 Infrastructure

To encourage the use of ICT, MSU has introduced a programe called Bring Your Own Device (BYOD). This has led to a rapid increase in the use of ICT in education. Under this programme students bring their own gadgets such as mobile phones, tablets and laptops and they connect to the internet. 46% of the interviewed lecturers indicated that when they gave out learning material, they assumed that students had gadgets that connected to the internet. However, is not always the case. Pondiwa and Phiri [13] argued that not all students have gadgets that are compatible with social media platforms and as such when learning materials are posted on social media such students may fail to access such material. The university has also invested so much in internet connectivity in all its campuses. There is Wi-Fi connectivity in all the campuses and learning centers. The university has promoted the use of interactive white boards instead of the traditional black boards. This has gone a long way in enabling a smart and conducive teaching and learning environment.

7.1.5 Library E resources

The university library has e resources and this has assisted students in a number of ways. They can access the library from anywhere for as long as they are connected to the internet. The Midlands State University has various electronic resources in the institutional repository. The MSU institutional repository is a platform where students and lecturers post their research material for others to access. This has gone a long way to promote knowledge sharing. This is a departure from the traditional approach where books and papers could only be physically accessed.

7.1.6 Policy

The use of ICT in education should be regulated by an official policy in order to yield good results. The study indicated that there was no explicit policy on the integration of ICT in education at both SUZA and MSU until the outbreak of Covid19. Before that, the choice of what to share on social media is left to the lecturer. On the issue of the use of social media as a learning and teaching platform, [13] posit that as at 2019 MSU did not have a policy that stipulated how social media could be used in education.

7.2 SUZA

7.2.1 Lectures and courses

At SUZA, depending on a degree and a semester the students are in, there are a number of compulsory courses that students have to take. Unfortunately, not all of these compulsory courses integrate the use of ICTs fully such as the usage of the Moodle platform. At SUZA the School of Education has the highest number of students. This is because majority of the students specializing in other fields such as

Sciences, IT and Arts have to take compulsory educational courses if they want to pursue the teaching profession after graduating. Other courses that are compulsory and have to be taken by all students regardless of the degrees they are doing are Communication Skills and Development Studies. These two courses have integrated ICT in teaching and learning.

7.2.2 Infrastructure and the use of e-learning

The State University of Zanzibar has taken major efforts in terms of infrastructure to ensure that ICT is integrated in education. There is a computer lab with internet connection at each campus to ensure that those students who do not have personal ICT devices are connected and can use the computers and internet for their learning. There is also free Wi-Fi across the university's 9 campuses to allow both the instructors and students to be connected to the internet through their mobile devices. The university has also introduced a Center for Digital Learning which works directly with the instructors and students in terms of producing educational videos for the SUZA TV. The Center for Digital Learning also conducts trainings on how to use e-learning and it also modifies and produces OERs and Kiswahili MOOCs. Despite all of these infrastructural efforts that have been taken by SUZA, there are still challenges that are faced by both instructors and students. The main shortcomings include poor internet connectivity. The other shortcomings are that sometimes there is no internet connection at all, power cuts, and the number of computer labs are enough to cater for all the users. Only 41% of the students can access these computer labs.

7.2.3 Policy

While there is an ICT policy, not everyone is aware of it. Until the outbreak of Coivd19 which made it almost impossible to attend physical lectures during the lockdown, SUZA did not have an explicit policy that regulated the use of social media in teaching and learning. Only 20% of the instructors indicated to be aware of the ICT policy at SUZA. The rest of the respondents have no idea of its existence. This simply shows that even if the course instructors or the students do not integrate ICT in their teaching and learning they will not be asked to explain why. On the other hand, the university does not motivate those who integrate ICT into education thus integration is at the discretion of the lecturer. Despite the fact that majority are unaware of the ICT policy, the results indicate that both instructors and students are aware of the benefits that come with the integration of ICT in teaching and learning. Instructors (65%) indicated that they integrate ICT into their teaching due to the fact that ICT allows them to engage with students directly. 88% indicated that they were getting reliable content online through Open Educational Resources Students also understand the benefits that come with the integration of ICT in their learning. The main reasons given by students include having an "easy access to course materials like lecture notes", "understanding the concepts easily through watching videos on YouTube" and "staying updated with notification with other students through social media platform like WhatsApp class groups".

8. Challenges and opportunities

There are numerous opportunities that both MSU and SUZA can utilize to successfully implement ICT integration in education at a higher rate. These opportunities include the presence of the Learning Management System, which is an essential platform in e-learning. Availability of ICT experts in all the campuses at the two institutions is another opportunity that could change the rate of ICT integration in education. The majority of students at SUZA (71%) and 87% at MSU indicated that they were keen in using technologies for learning. The research indicated that there are some barriers that hinder the integration of ICT in education at both MSU and SUZA include lack of confidence, lack of competence in the use of computers, lack of electricity, lack of funding and lack of access to resources. It should be recommended that ICT resources including software and hardware, effective professional development, sufficient time, and technical support need to be addressed if integration is to be effective [3].

9. Discussion

This research revealed that at both MSU and SUZA, the use of ICT in Education has been adopted and has yielded a number of results. This has had an impact on teaching and learning. Similarly, while studying integration of ICT in education in Asia, [4] observed that Asian institutions that have utilized ICT effectively, have changed the way lecturers/teachers and administrators approach curriculum delivery.

9.1 Infrastructure

Integration of ICT requires a lot of Government and institutional support. 40% of Lecturers interviewed at MSU indicated that when they tried to integrate ICT own their own, they had faced many challenges. Some of these challenges stemmed from the fact that the institution does not have an explicit policy on when and how the ICT can be integrated. Most efforts during the first years of integration came from lecturers who were keen on the use of ICT. The research indicated that there is need for university management to commit themselves through policies and the provision of funds to ensure that there is adequate infrastructure and the human resources that enable effective integration of ICT into education. The problem of electricity was also found to be common at SUZA. This was also confirmed by an earlier study by [6]. A very important requirement of ICT is the availability of a stable supply of electricity and internet connectivity. The MSU has standby generators at all its campuses but these are very expensive to run such that at times when there is no electricity from the national supplier, the university has not been able to switch on all the generators. This has affected lesson delivery especially in cases where a lecturer would have planned to use ICT to deliver the lecture. The ICT Director at MSU when asked what Challenges the institution was facing in its efforts to integrate ICT in education he commented, "The greatest challenge is that of electricity supply When there is a blackout this also affects internet connectivity. All our efforts to fully integrate are being hampered by the constant power outages. This has forced lecturers to go back to the black board, something we have been trying to move away from".

9.2 Training in ICT

At both MSU and SUZA not all lecturers are formally trained in the use of ICT, resulting in students losing out because of the limitation on the part of the lecturer. 30% of the lecturers interviewed at MSU and 41% at SUZA indicated that they had not received any training on the use of the ICT gadgets such as the interactive boards which the university acquired. This, according to the University administration at MSU, had a serious impact on the university's efforts to have fully integrated ICT in all teaching and learning activities by the end of 2023. (MSU Strategic Plan 2018–2023) During a Risk Management committee meeting on 17 October 2019, the chairperson lamented the abuse of the interactive white boards by both students and lecturers. He indicated that there had been the use of sharp objects on the interactive board and this had affected the sensitivity of the boards as they could not properly function due to this abuse. This is indication that while there can be infrastructure; lack of training on how to utilize it can also hamper its effectiveness.

Despite the availability of ICT labs, not every student has had access to ICT based teaching material as most of them do not have gadgets that are compatible with the provided ICT infrastructure. Some do not have smart phones. Interviews indicated that when a lecturer posts material on social media platforms not everyone has access. Pondiwa and Phiri [13] argued that when lecturers use social media as a teaching and learning platform, there is an assumption is that everyone has access to gadgets that are compatible with social media platforms.

10. Benefits of ICT integration into education

This study indicated that new technologies spur spontaneous interest more than tradition approaches of learning. Both Lecturers and students from the two institutions indicated that they would prefer the use of ICT in education. 78% of students who answered questionnaire questions indicated that they would prefer to have lectures and other teaching material delivered using ICT. One learner from the MSU Harare campus indicated that instead of lecturers having to travel to campus they could just use ICT facilities such as Google class, Skype or the E- learning accounts of students to deliver teaching and learning material.

ICT promotes collaborative and cooperative learning. This happens when there is interaction and cooperation among teachers and students regardless of distance. ICT increases contact among learners and facilitates the level of communication between these students and their lecturers. The results from this research indicated that as numbers of students increase, lecturers find it convenient to adopt ICT as it becomes difficult to have personal contacts with the students. This is confirmed by Lau-rillard1994 who posits that ICT provides opportunities for departments, faculties and college and universities to communicate relatively easily.

ICT promotes creative learning in that it gives students greater chances of being independent and this gives them room to be innovative. Students at both MSU and SUZA confirmed that the adoption of ICT in learning has given them the independence in that if one misses a lecture they can still catch up if the learning material is posted on their e-learning accounts or other platforms such as Google class, WhatsApp and Facebook. The adoption of e learning provides institutions of learning such as SUZA and MSU with flexibility of time and place of delivery or receipt of learning information. Traditional teaching methods are relatively more expensive than the modern ones. One reason traditional teaching cost more than e-learning is because it involves more staff expenses. Faculties that used ICT had fewer teaching assistants as compared to those departments who used traditional ways of teaching. A departmental chairperson when interviewed commented that with the introduction of e-learning, the need for someone to always physically attend lecturers was now a thing of the past as it was now possible to post learning material on e-learning portals and students would access even without getting to the lecture room.

11. Conclusion

The study indicated that there has been massive integration of ICT in education at both MSU and SUZA. The integration of ICT into education, though faced with many challenges, has improved teaching and learning in a number of ways. The integration of ICT into education is an area that still needs a lot of commitment and investment if it is to yield better results. There is also need to continuously improve ICT infrastructure as it is ever changing.

Author details

Shephard Pondiwa[1*], Umayra El Nabahany[2] and Margaret Phiri[1]

1 Midlands State University, Gweru, Zimbabwe

2 State University of Zanzibar, SUZA, Zanzibar, Tanzania

*Address all correspondence to: pondiwas@gmail.com

IntechOpen

© 2021 The Author(s). Licensee IntechOpen. This chapter is distributed under the terms of the Creative Commons Attribution License (http://creativecommons.org/licenses/by/3.0), which permits unrestricted use, distribution, and reproduction in any medium, provided the original work is properly cited. (cc) BY

References

[1] El Nabahany U, Mosbech, M Mgeni and Yunus, S (2019), Transformation into Digitally supported Education: Case from State University of Zanzibar. In: Tatnall A., Mavengere N. (eds) Sustainable ICT, Education and Learning. SUZA 2019. IFIP Advances in Information and Communication Technology, vol 564. Springer, Cham

[2] Grabe, M., and Grabe, C. (2007). Integrating technology for meaningful learning (5th ed.). Boston, MA: Houghton Mifflin

[3] Ghavifekr S and W Rosdy (2015), Teaching and learning with technology. Effectiveness of ICT integration in schools, Journal of research in education and science.

[4] Wong G.K.W (2015) Understanding technology acceptance in pre-service teachers of pri-mary mathematics in Hong Kong the Hong Kong Institute of Education, Australasian Jour-nal of Educational Technology, 2015, 31(6).

[5] Kachembere, J. (2011). ICT boom: Zimbabwe's opportunity to catch-up. The Standard Zim-babwe. Retrieved 13 December 2019, http:www.thestandard.co.zw/index.php.

[6] El Nabahany U and Juma S, (2019), Integrating ICT in pre service Teacher Education in Zanzibar, Status, Challenges and opportunities In: Tatnall A., Mavengere N. (eds) Sustaina-ble ICT, Education and Learning. SUZA 2019. IFIP Advances in Information and Commu-nication Technology, vol 564. Springer, Cham

[7] Isaacs, S. (2007) Survey of ICT and Education in Africa: South Africa country, Re-port. Info Dev ICT and education series. World Bank, Washington, DC.

[8] Lee, Y, Kozar, K.A. and Larsen, Kai. (2003). The Technology Acceptance Model: Past, Present, and Future. Technology. 12. 10.17705/1CAIS.01250.

[9] Yin, R. K. (2009). Case study research: Design and methods (4th Ed.). Thousand Oaks, CA: Sage

[10] Musarurwa C (2011) Teaching with and Learning through ICT in Zimbabwe's Teacher ed-ucation colleges Yin, R. K. (2009). Case study research: Design and methods (4th Ed.). Thousand Oaks, CA: Sage

[11] Richard H and Haya A (2009) Examining student decision to adopt Web 2.0 Technologies: Theory and Empirical tests, Journal of computing in higher education.

[12] Yunus. S. A. S, Abudulla. A. A, Ahamda. R. I, U. El-Nabhany and P. Malliga (2019) The integration of Web 2.0 in Teaching-Learning in Tanzania Higher Learning Institutions: The case study of The State University of Zanzibar (SUZA)

[13] Pondiwa S., and Phiri M. (2019) Challenges and Opportunities of Managing Social Media Generated Records in Institutions of Learning: A Case of the Midlands State University, Zimbabwe. In: Tatnall A., Mavengere N. (eds) Sustainable ICT, Education and Learning. SUZA 2019. IFIP Advances in Information and Communication Technology, vol 564. Springer, Cham